AS PER THE NEW SYLLABUS PRESCRIBED BY THE DEPARTMENT OF ECONOMICS, M.D. UNIVERSITY ROHTAK FOR THE M.A. ECONOMICS (FIVE YEAR INTEGRATED COURSE) AND B.A. ECONOMICS (HONS.) EFFECTIVE FROM JULY 2013

FUNDAMENTALS OF HUMAN RESOURCE DEVELOPMENT

DR. SUBHASH

(M.A., M.Phil., Ph.D.)

FUNDAMENTALS OF HUMAN RESOURCE DEVELOPMENT
Author: DR. SUBHASH

■

RED'SHINE PUBLICATION PVT. LTD.

Headquarters (India): 88, Patel Street, Navamuvada,
Lunawada, India-389 230

Contact: +91 76988 26988

Registration no. GJ31D0000034

In Association with,

RED'MAC INTERNATIONAL PRESS & MEDIA. INC

India | Sweden | Canada

■

Text © DR. SUBHASH, 2019

Cover page ©RED'SHINE Studios, Inc, 2019

■

■

ISBN: 978-93-87822-98-6 (softcover)

Price: ₹ 250

DIP: 18.10.986/87822

February, 2019 (First Edition)

■

■

www.redshine.co.in | info.redmac@gmail.com

Printed in India | Title ID: 87822986

Dedicated to

Bhavna, Abhinav and Aarav

ACKNOWLEDGEMENT

First and foremost I offer my sincere thanks to the hundreds of undergraduate and postgraduate students who have taken and participated in my Lectures in Economics over the past twelve years. Without these students of Economics I would never have been faced with the challenge to write this book. The students have been the real motivators for writing this piece of work. My special thanks to Dr. B. R. Ambedkar, The Father of The Indian Constitution who has been my real emancipator and a true guide throughout my academic journey.

This book could not have been possible without collaborative efforts and support of my colleagues at Dronacharya Govt. College Gurugram, Haryana, India. My special thanks to Prof. Bhup Singh, Head of the Dept., Sociology who always inspires me to do research work, papers presentation in seminars and writing of books/articles/papers etc. I am also very thankful to my colleagues and friends Dr. Sudhir Samantrai, Dr. Mool Chand, Ms. Nitasha Joon, Shri Sandeep Yadav, Dr. Sushil K. Saini, Dr. Karamvir, Dr. Garima Yadav, Sachin, Dr. Sunita and Ms. Renu who helped me directly or indirectly at many occasions in the college.

I express my thanks to the head of the dept. Economics, Shri R.M.S. Yadav who provided me freedom in selecting the papers to teach. I would also like to acknowledge the help, encouragement and support received from my seniors and friends of BANISS, MHOW— Azhagnathan, R.K. Chauhan and P.K.Janoliya.

My heartfelt thanks to the Redshine Publications Pvt. Ltd. who agreed to publish this book on a reasonable price. I would like to thanks Dr. Vishal Parmar and his team for making a very attractive cover-design for this book.

Last but not the least, I express my heartfelt thanks to my wife Bhavna Hammad who continuously supported and encouraged me. Smile of my little champs Abhinav and Aarav has always been refreshing and energetic for me during this entire piece of work. Thank you! My little Champs.

JANUARY, 2019   **Dr. Subhash**

(M.A., M.Phil., Ph.D.)

PREFACE

This book on HRD is a product of many years of my teaching and learning experience at different UG and PG Govt. colleges in the state of Haryana. There is no such book of *Human Resource Development* available in the market where students of B.A. Economics (Hons.) & M.A. can find the whole syllabus for the preparation of final examinations. Students have to consult a number of books, papers, articles, journals etc. to cover the entire course of study of *Human Resource Development* for B. A. Economics (Hons.) Semester-VI. This necessitated the publication of this book entitled- *'Fundamentals of Human Resource Development* so that students can have entire course of study at one place. Students from rural areas will find it very comfortable as language used in this book is very simple and clear. The contribution of some eminent scholars like- Nadler, Swanson, Monika Lee, T. V. Rao and M. N. Khan has immensely influenced my understanding and interest in the subject of HRD. The book describes traditional as well as modern developments in HRD. I am sure this book will be highly valuable to the teachers, students and HRD practitioners.

Some important features of the book are as follows:

1 *A comprehensive coverage of the entire syllabus at one place.*

2 *The exposition of the text is clear and precise.*

3 *The analysis in each chapter has been developed step by step in a systematic manner.*

4 *Presentation and explanation of the concepts are simple, clear and easy.*

5 *A list of recommended books for advanced learning.*

I shall value immensely any suggestions of the teachers, students and HRD practitioners for the improvement of this book.

January, 2019   **Dr. Subhash**

DGC-Gurugram   *(M.A., M.Phil., Ph.D.)*

SYLLABUS

B.A.- VI Sem., MDU-Rohtak VI .2
HUMAN RESOURCE DEVELOPMENT

Max. Marks: 100   Written Exam: 80
Time: 3 Hrs.   Internal Assessment: 20

Course Outcomes:

CO1: The course will explain significant concepts and theories underpinning HRD.

CO2: Students would develop skills in identifying HRD needs and in designing, implementing and evaluating HRD programs.

CO3: Students would be able to Critically analyse and evaluate contemporary HRD practices.

UNIT-I

Human Resource Development (HRD): Concept, nature, scope, significance, objectives, functions; Traditional and modern approaches; Human Resource Development and Manpower Planning.

UNIT-II

Human Capital: Concept of human capital and its determinants, problems of measurement; An appraisal of underlying theories of Human capital formation particularly in the context of developing Economies; Role of public and private investment in human capital formation; Economics of education (formal, informal, on-the-job training and re-training, An introduction to economics of health and nutrition.

UNIT-III

Functioning of Market for Human Resources: Internal allocation and brain drain, asymmetric information and functioning of the human resource market; Migration

(Theories, and the emerging challenges); Managing Human Resources (wages, incentives- productivity relationship, economics of discrimination).

UNIT-IV

Human Resource Management Practices: Human Resource Management in developed countries, and India (in Public Enterprises and small undertakings); Emerging human resource management concepts and systems in the new millennium; Human Resource Information System.

NOTE : The question paper shall have five units. Each of the first four units will contain two questions and the students shall be asked to attempt one question from each unit. Unit five shall contain eight to ten short answer type questions without any internal choice and it shall be covering the entire syllabus. As such, unit five shall be compulsory

CONTENTS

CHAPTER - 1
HUMAN RESOURCE DEVELOPMENT: MEANING AND DEFINITION

INTRODUCTION

Of all the factors of production, human is by far the most important. The importance of human factor in any type of co-operative endeavor cannot be overemphasized. It is a matter of common knowledge that every business organization depends for its effective functioning not so much on its material or financial resources as on its pool of able and willing human resources. The product of any manufacturing organization by itself is not enough to win customers. The human resources become even more important in service industry whose value is delivered through information, personal interaction or group work. This is the only resource which can produce unlimited amounts through better ideas. There is no apparent limit to what people can accomplish when they are motivated to use their potential to create new and better ideas. No other resource can do this.

The origins of HRD are widely contested among researchers and across geographic and cultural boundaries. However, in the United States, the Industrial Revolution is recognized once again as a driving force in the evolution of HRD. Like Taylor, Henry Ford sought to improve the efficiency of his operations by mitigating the impact of human resources. Ford designed a production process that utilized the most efficient movements and maximized employee capabilities. The Ford assembly line is a notable contribution to low design and lean management in today's operations. By the mid-1930s, the formal concept of organizational development (OD) emerged.

The theories supporting OD drove ongoing employee training and development opportunities (Haslinda, 2009; Stewart & Sambrook, 2012). Similarly, World War II led to the increased need for employee training to produce warships and military equipment, which employees were not previously apt at doing.In the late 1950s, psychology introduced the human element to OD. Theories on effective employee development activities rose to the forefront of management concern. Psychologists, Argyris, McGregor, Likert, and Herzberg popularized the notion that employee development activities directly influence employee performance.

In 1970, Leonard Nadler published his book "Developing Human Resources" in which he coined the term 'human resource development' (HRD). Human resource refers to the talents and energies of people that are available to an organization as potential contributors to the creation and realization of the organization's mission, vision, values, and goals.

Development refers to a process of active learning from experience-leading to systematic and purposeful development of the whole person, body, mind, and spirit. Thus, HRD is the integrated use of training, organizational and career development efforts to improve individual, group, and organizational effectiveness.

Human Resource Development (HRD) can be formal such as in classroom training, a college course, or an organizational planned change effort. Or, Human Resource Development (HRD) can be informal as in employee coaching by a manager. Healthy organizations believe in Human Resource Development (HRD) and cover all of these bases.

Human Resource Development (HRD) is a process of developing skills, competencies, knowledge and attitudes of people in an organization. The people become human resource only when they are competent to perform organizational activities. Therefore, Human Resource Development (HRD) ensures that the organization has such competent human resource to achieve its desired goals and objectives. Human Resource Development (HRD) imparts the required knowledge and skill in them through effective arrangement of training and development programs. Human Resource Development (HRD) is an integral part of

Human Resource Management (HRM) which is more concerned with training and development, career planning and development and the organization development. The organization has to understand the dynamics of HR and attempt to cope with changing situation in order to deploy its HR effectively and efficiently. And Human Resource Development (HRD) helps to reach this target.

HUMAN RESOURCE DEVELOPMENT (HRD) - CONCEPT

Human Resource Development (HRD) is a positive concept as an area of managing human resources. It is based on the belief that it is imperative and constructive for an organization to invest in human beings to bring substantial benefits in the long run. It aims at the overall development of the human resource in order to contribute for the well-being of the employees, organization and the society at large. Out of the fundamental areas of Management, Human Resource Management is adjudged as the most important area of study and concern. In the Management of four M's i.e. Money, Machines, Materials and Men, the management of men is the most significant and challenging. The efficiency of the whole lot of activities carried out in an organization starting from the production process to the management of various areas of administration depends to a large extent on the level of Human Resource Development (HRD).

The paradigm of managing employees has undergone rapid transformation in the last decade, from comparative advantage to a state of continuous innovation, intelligent framework and strategic intent for competitive advantage. Today's personnel are more demanding and have high aspirations. They demand early up-gradation of their skills and competencies. This implies that the organizations should develop appropriate Human Resource Development (HRD) policies and take care in formulating and implementing such policies by keeping in mind the objective of the firm and integrating those objectives with that of the organization.

Human Resource Development (HRD) is rooted in the belief that human beings have the potential to do well. It therefore, secures a premium place for the dignity and tremendous latent energy and potential of people. Where the balance sheet shows people on the debit side, Human Resource Development (HRD) seeks to show them as 'assets' on the credit side. In the present era of liberalization and globalization Human Resource Development (HRD) is emerging as an interdisciplinary and integrated approach for the development of human resource.

Definitions of Human Resource Development (HRD):
HRD has numerous definitions. It would be good to reflect on alternate views of HRD so that students/practitioners are exposed to a range of thinking in the profession.

1. According to **South Pacific Commission** 'human resource development is equipping people with relevant skills to have a healthy and satisfying life'.

2. According to **Watkins,** 'human resource development is fostering long-term work related learning capacity at individual, group and organizational level'.

3. **The American Society for Training and Development** defines HRD as follows: 'human resource development is the process of increasing the capacity of the human resource through development. It is thus the process of adding value to individuals, teams or an organization as a human system'.

4. **Swanson (1987)** provides a popular definition: "HRD is a process of improving an organization performance through the capabilities of its personnel. HRD includes activities dealing with work design, aptitude, expertise, and motivation" (Swanson and Holton , 2008).

5. According to **Leonard Nadler**, "Human Resource Development (HRD) is a series of organised activities, conducted within a specialised time and designed to produce behavioural changes."

6. **T.V. Rao** the best known Indian HRD expert who is regarded as the Father of Indian HRD, defined "HRD as a process in which the employees of an organization are continuously helped in a planned way to:

    i) acquire or sharpen their capabilities required to perform various obligations, tasks and functions associated with and related to their present or future expected roles;

    ii) develop their capabilities as individuals so that they may be able to discover their potentialities and exploit them to the full for their own and/or organizational development purposes; and

    iii) to develop an organizational culture where superior subordinate relationships, team work and collaboration among different sub-units are strong and contribute to the organizational wealth, dynamism and pride of the employees."

T.V. Rao views that the main objective of HRD is to facilitate the growth and development of a manager in the organization in a planned way. (Rao, 2012).

7.	According to **Harbison and Myers** -"HRD is the process of increasing the knowledge, capacities of all the people, and skills in a society. From the economic point of view the term could be described as the accumulation of human capital and its effective investment in the development of an economy. In political terms, HRD prepares people for adult participation in the political process, particularly as citizens in a democracy. From the social and cultural view, the development of human resource helps people lead fuller and richer lives as well as to be less bound to tradition. In brief, the processes of HRD unlock the door to modernization."

8.	**Khan M. N.** remarked "HRD is the process of increasing knowledge, skills, capabilities and positive work attitudes and values of all people working at all levels in a business undertaking." (Khan, 1987).

Features of HRD:

1. Systematic approach:

HRD is a systematic and planned approach through which the efficiency of employees is improved. The future goals and objectives are set by the entire organization, which are well planned at individual and organizational levels.

2. Continuous process:

HRD is a continuous process for the development of all types of skills of employees such as technical, managerial, behavioural, and conceptual. Till the retirement of an employee sharpening of all these skills is required.

3. Multi-disciplinary subject:

HRD is a Multi-disciplinary subject which draws inputs from behavioural science, engineering, commerce, management, economics, medicine, etc.

4. All-pervasive:

HRD is an essential subject everywhere, be it a manufacturing organization or service sector industry.

5. Techniques:

HRD embodies with techniques and processes such as performance appraisal, training, management development, career planning, counselling, workers' participation and quality circles.

■

CHAPTER – 2

HUMAN RESOURCE DEVELOPMENT (HRD)-NATURE, SCOPE, OBJECTIVES, IMPORTANCE AND FUNCTION

NATURE of HRD

1. **Continuous Process** - Human Resource Development (HRD) is a continuous process.
2. **Behavioural Knowledge** - Human Resource Development (HRD) concerned with behavioural knowledge.
3. **Integrated** - Human Resource Development (HRD) is a well integrated system.
4. Human Resource Development (HRD) provides better quality of life.
5. **All Round Development** - Human Resource Development (HRD) focuses on all round development of human resources.

SCOPE OF HUMAN RESOURCE DEVELOPMENT

HRD is broader than human resource management; it consists of several sub-systems such as training and development, employee appraisal, counseling, rewards and welfare, quality of work life, etc. these are the areas within its scope.

The following topics are included within the scope of HRD:

1. **Training**: - Training is an essential element of HRD. This develops skills and capacity to work at higher levels and positions. Training is possible by different methods. It is useful for self-development and career development.

2. **Performance appraisal**: - Performance appraisal is an important area of HRD. The purpose of performance appraisal is to study critically the performance of an employee and to guide him to improve his performance. This technique is useful for building a team of capable employees and is also used for their self-development.

3. **Potential appraisal**: - It relates to the study of capabilities of employees. It is useful for proper placement and career development of employees. Potential appraisal of employees is useful for developing their special qualities, which can be used fruitfully along with the expansion and diversification of activities of the company.

4. **Career planning and development**: - Under HRD employees should be given guidance for their self-development and career development. The opportunities likely to develop in the organization should be brought to their notice. They should be motivated for self-development, which is useful to the organization in the long run.

5. **Employees' welfare**: - Employees welfare is within the scope of HRD. Welfare facilities are useful for creating efficient and satisfied labour force. Such facilities raise the morale of employees. Employee welfare include the provision of medical and recreation facilities, subsidized canteen, free raining and other measures introduced for HRD.

6. **Rewards and incentives**: - HRD includes provision of rewards and incentives to employees to encourage them to learn, to grow and to develop new qualities, skills and experiences which will be useful in the near future. Reward is an appreciation of good work. It may be in the form of promotion, higher pay etc.

7. **Organizational development**: - HRD aims at providing conflict-free operations throughout the organization. It also keeps plans ready to deal with problems like absenteeism, turnover, low productivity or industrial disputes.

8. **Quality of work life**: - Quality of work life depends on sound relations between employer (owner) and employees. A forward looking policy on employee benefits like job security, attractive pay, participative management and monetary and non-monetary rewards will go a long way in improving the quality of work life.

9. **Human resource information system**: - Such system acts as information bank and facilitates human resource planning and development in a proper manner. It facilitates quick decision-making in regard to HRD. Every organization has to introduce such system for ready reference to HRD matters.

10. Development of employees through managerial and behavioural skills.

Objectives of HRD:

The prime objective of human resource development is to facilitate an organizational environment in which the people come first. The other objectives of HRD are as follows:

1. Equity:

Recognizing every employee at par irrespective of caste, creed, religion and language, can create a very good environment in an organization. HRD must ensure that the organization creates a culture and provides equal opportunities to all employees in matters of career planning, promotion, quality of work life, training and development.

2. Employability:

Employability means the ability, skills, and competencies of an individual to seek gainful employment anywhere. So, HRD should aim at improving the skills of employees in order to motivate them to work with effectiveness.

3. Adaptability:

Continuous training that develops the professional skills of employees plays an important role in HRD. This can help the employees to adapt themselves to organizational change that takes place on a continuous basis.

Bhattacharya stated objectives of HRD as

1. "To develop capabilities of each individual in an organization/institution in relation to his/her present role.
2. To develop capabilities of each individual in relation to his/her future role.
3. To develop better interpersonal and employer-employee relationship in an organization.
4. To develop team spirit.
5. To develop coordination among different units of an organization/institution.
6. Facilitate organization/institution to utilize human resources effectively by providing them training and orientation.
7. Help manpower planning and prevent over staffing
8. Provide opportunity for people/staff as career advancement path.
9. It helps to increase motivation level of people/staff.
10. To develop organizational health by continuous renewal of individual capabilities and keeping pace with the technological changes.
11. The objectives of HRD practices in an organization should be to encourage efforts in the workforce, including

management and to maintain an environment conductive to total participation, leadership and personal along with organizational growth. In an organization there are six units which are concerned with HRD, namely person, role, dyad, team, inter-team and organization. The effectiveness of one contributes in turn to effectiveness of others."

Importance of Human Resource Development (HRD)

Human resource is needed to be developed as per the change in external environment of the organization, hence, HRD helps to adapt such changes through the development of existing human resource in terms of skill and knowledge.

The importance or significance of HRD can be explained as follows:

1. HRD Develops Competent HR

HRD develops the skills and knowledge of individuals. Hence, it helps to provide competent and efficient HR as per the job requirement. To develop employment's skill and competencies, different **training and development** programs are launched.

2. HRD Creates Opportunity for Career Development

HRD helps to grasp the career development opportunities through development of human skills and knowledge. **Career development** consists of personal development efforts through a proper match between training and development opportunities with employee's need.

3. Employ Commitment

Trained and efficient employees are committed towards their jobs which is possible through HRD. If employees are provided with proper training and development opportunities, they will feel committed to the work and the organization.

4. Job Satisfaction

When people in the organization are well oriented and developed, they show higher degree of commitment in actual work place. This inspires them for better performance, which ultimately leads to **job satisfaction**.

5. Change Management

HRD facilitates planning, and management of change in an organization. It also manages conflicts through improved labor management relation. It develops organizational health, culture and environment which lead to change management.

6. Opportunities For Training And Development

Trainings and development programs are tools of HRD. They provide opportunity for employee's development by matching training needs with organizational requirement. Moreover, HRD facilitates integrated growth of employees through training and development activities.

7. Performance Improvement

HRD develops necessary skills and abilities required to perform organizational activities. As a result of which, employees can contribute for better performance in an organization. This leads to greater organizational effectiveness.

HRD Functions:

HRD functions include the following:

1. **Employee training and development:**

Training and development is one of the key HRD functions. Most organisations look at training and development as an integral part of the human resource development activity. The turn of the century has seen increased focus on the same in organisations globally. Many organisations have mandated training hours per year for employees keeping in consideration the fact that technology is deskilling the employees at a very fast rate. Technically training involves change in attitude, skills or knowledge of a person with the resultant improvement in the behaviour.

Development implies opportunities created to help employees grow. It is more of long term or futuristic in nature as opposed to training, which focus on the current job. It also is not limited to the job avenues in the current organisation but may focus on other development aspects also. The major difference between training and development therefore is that while training focuses often on the current employee needs or competency gaps, development concerns itself with preparing people for future assignments and responsibilities.

2. Career planning and development

Career planning is an ongoing process through which an individual sets career goals and identifies the means to achieve them. The process by which individuals plan their life's work is referred to as career planning. Career is viewed as a sequence of position occupied by a person during the course of his lifetime. Career may also be viewed as amalgam of changes in value, attitude and motivation that occur, as a person grows older. The implicit assumption is that an individual can make a different in his destiny over time and can adjust in ways that would help him to enhance and optimize the potential for his own career development. Career planning is important because it would help the individual to explore, choose and strive to derive satisfaction with one's career object.

3. Succession planning

Succession planning is a process for identifying and developing new leaders who can replace old leaders when they leave, retire or die. Succession planning increases the availability of experienced and capable employees that are prepared to assume these roles as they become available. Taken narrowly, "replacement planning" for key roles is the heart of succession planning. Effective succession planning works by assessing staffing needs that may arise and creating long-term goals and strategies to manage those gaps, including through leadership development. The HR department, sometimes referred to as the *human resources management department*, is typically a key driver in the succession planning, which is sometimes referred to as *replacement planning*, although support from top leadership and other stakeholders is critical to success.

4. Performance appraisal

Performance Appraisal is the systematic evaluation of the performance of employees and to understand the abilities of a person for further growth and development. Performance appraisal is generally done in systematic ways which are as follows: 1) The supervisors measure the pay of employees and compare it with targets and plans, 2) The supervisor analyses the factors behind work performances of employees and 3) The employers are in a position to guide the employees for a better performance.

5. Employee's participation in management

Workers' participation in management implies mental and emotional involvement of workers in the management of Enterprise. It is considered as a mechanism where workers have a say in the decision making. Workers' participation in management is an essential ingredient of Industrial democracy. The concept of workers' participation in management is based on Human Relations approach to Management which brought about a new set of values to labour and management. Traditionally the concept of Workers' Participation in Management (WPM) refers to participation of non-managerial employees in the decision-making process of the organization. Workers' participation is also known as 'labour participation' or 'employee participation' in management. In Germany it is known as co-determination while in Yugoslavia it is known as self-management. The International Labour Organization has been encouraging member nations to promote the scheme of Workers' Participation in Management

6. Quality circles

A quality circle is a volunteer group composed of workers , usually under the leadership of their supervisor , who are trained to identify, analyze and solve work-related problems and present their solutions to management in order to improve the performance of the organization, and motivate and enrich the work of employees. When matured, true quality circles become self-managing and gained the confidence of management.

Participative management technique within the framework of a company wise quality system in which small teams of (usually 6 to 12) employees voluntarily form to define and solve a quality or performance related problem. In Japan (where this practice originated) quality circles are an integral part of enterprise management and are called quality control circles.

7. Organization change and organization development.

Internal and external changes affect the organization as a whole. It is the organization's responsibility to provide its workforce the necessary knowledge and skills that will take advantage of the opportunities and steer clear of the threats. A well-informed, well-trained workforce leads to the efficiency in the operations of the organization and is able to focus the activities of the organization towards achieving its objectives.

The capabilities of the workforce directly impact the organization as they give the organization competitive edge. Due to internal and external changes, the organization must adapt to these changes to avoid revenue loss. To adapt to these changes, the HRD department conducts training with the goal of improving on the capabilities of the organization's employees. This training is referred to as the HRD. The goal of HRD is to improve the skills and knowledge of the employees towards achieving the objectives of the organization.

Traditional Vs Modern Human Resource Development

The major difference between "Traditional HRD" and "Modern HRD" is that; the Traditional Approach is the Personnel development whereas the Modern Approach is the Human Resource development toward managing people in an enterprise.

	Traditional HRD	**Modern HRD**
Meaning	It is a predominantly administrative record-keeping function that aims to establish and maintain equitable terms and conditions of employment.	It integrates the traditional personnel management functions to corporate goals and strategies, and performs additional people centered organizational developmental activities.
Scope	1 Narrow Scope 2. It include functional activities such as;-Manpower planning, -Recruitment, -Job analysis,-Job Evaluation,-Payroll Administration,-Performance Appraisals,-Labor Law Compliance,-Training Administration. Etc	1.Broader Scope 2.It includes all these activities plus Organizational Developmental activities such as;-Leadership,-Motivation,-Developing Organizational Culture,-Communication of Shared Values.Etc. 3.These approaches remains integrated to the company's core strategy, vision, and seek to optimize the use of human resource for the fulfillment of organizational goals. 4.The strategic and philosophical context of human resource management makes it more purposeful, relevant, and more effective compared to the personnel management (traditional approach)
Approach	It gives importance to;-Norms,- Customs-, Established practices	It gives importance;-Values-, Mission

	Traditional HRD	**Modern HRD**
Nature	1. It remains aloof from core organizational activities and functions. 2. It takes an immediate approach to bring changes in corporate goals or strategies	1. It remains integrated with corporate strategy and takes a proactive approach to align the workforce toward achievement of corporate goals. 2. It has a more comprehensive and proactive performance management system that aims to correct performance rather than make a report card of past performance
Application	It is an independent staff function of an organization, with little involvement from line managers, and no linkage to the organizations core process. 2.It endeavors to reconcile the goals and views of the workforce with management interest by institutional means.	1.It carries out much of the human resource management tasks; it involves the line management and operations staff heavily. 2.It gives greater thrust on dealing with each employee independently and gives more importance to customer-focused developmental activities.

■

CHAPTER – 3
MANPOWER PLANNING: MEANING, STEPS AND IMPORTANCE

Manpower planning is the process of estimating the optimum number of people required for completing a project, task or a goal within time. Manpower planning includes parameters like number of personnel, different types of skills, time period etc. It is a never ending continuous process to make sure that the business has the optimized resources available when required taking into consideration the upcoming future projects and also the replacement of the outgoing employees. It is also called as Human Resource Planning.

Manpower Planning which is also called as Human Resource Planning consists of putting right number of people, right kind of people at the right place, right time, doing the right things for which they are suited for the achievement of goals of the organization. Human Resource Planning has got an important place in the arena of industrialization.

Planning is forward-looking — a mental exercise with the element of forecasting. Man-power consisting of the number of personnel, their physical capabilities, mental abilities, their attainments and attitudes to work has to be planned judiciously embracing all these aspects to achieve the desired goals of the organisation. Within the framework of overall business plan are the divisional and functional plans and the man-power planning is the branch of personnel function.

Example of Manpower Planning:

IT companies are often faced with the business problem of hiring right people for upcoming projects as well as attrition.

These companies have multiple projects going on at a single time and upcoming projects in the pipeline. If they hire more people without planning they would end up with many resources on the bench which would eat into profits and if they keep waiting till the last, they would not have enough skilled people to set up the project and start delivering eventually leading to customer dissatisfaction and losses.

So these companies keep on forecasting and planning as per the market requirements, latest skill set and their project pipeline. Most of the times, hired resources cannot be productive straight away so they need to train them which would require further planning and time.

Definitions

1. **According to Gorden MacBeath**, manpower planning involves two stages. The first stage is concerned with the detailed "planning of manpower requirements for all types and levels of employees throughout the period of the plan," and the second stage is concerned with "planning of manpower supplies to provide the organisation with the right types of people from all sources to meet the planned requirements."

2. **According to Vetter,** the process by which management determines how the organisation should move from its current manpower position to its desired manpower position. Through planning, management strives to have the right number and the right kinds of people, at the right places, at the right time, doing things which result in both the organisation and the individual receiving maximum long-run benefit.

3. **Coleman** has defined human resource or manpower planning as "the process of determining manpower requirements and the means for meeting those

requirements in order to carry out the integrated plan of the organisation."

4. **Stainer** defines manpower planning as "Strategy for the acquisition, utilisation, improvement, and preservation of an enterprise's human resources. It relates to establishing job specifications or the quantitative requirements of jobs determining the number of personnel required and developing sources of manpower."

5. According to **Wickstrom,** human resource planning consists of a series of activities, viz: (a) Forecasting future manpower requirements, either in terms of mathematical projections of trends in the economic environment and development in industry, or in terms of judgmental estimates based upon the specific future plans of a company; (b) Making an inventory of present manpower resources and assessing the extent to which these resources are employed optimally; (c) Anticipating manpower problems by projecting present resources into the future and comparing them with the forecast of requirements to determine their adequacy, both quantitatively and qualitatively; and (d) Planning the necessary programmes of requirement, selection, training, development, utilization, transfer, promotion, motivation and compensation to ensure that future manpower requirements are properly met.

Manpower Planning Process

HRD department of every company has to constantly keep an eye on the human resources that the company has. With every possible event like change industry dynamics, increase in business requirements, skills required for a particular technology etc, the need for having better resources increases. The process and steps for having manpower planning are as below:

1. Understanding the existing workforce: The HR department has to thoroughly understand the manpower available with the company. They should examine the background, skill set, qualification, location etc of the entire work force so that they have a good idea regarding the pool of talent which the company has.

2. Forecasting for the future: With constant changes in business requirements, companies must understand the future trend and which type of employees would be best suited for their organization. Hence, companies must examine, evaluate and forecast the type of employee workforce they want in the future years

3. Recruitment and selection: Depending upon the business requirements, manpower planning leads to a much more well thought out recruitment and selection pattern. This totally depends upon the forecasts made and the business requirements. Hence, candidates with better qualification, skill set, experience etc are shortlisted as employees to best suit the future needs.

4. Training the employees: Employees who are a part of the organization are trained to have the best skills, knowledge and understanding about the current job as well as the future requirements.

All these above mentioned manpower planning steps help organizations become better prepared to adapt to new technology, future industry developments and even to face off with competitors.

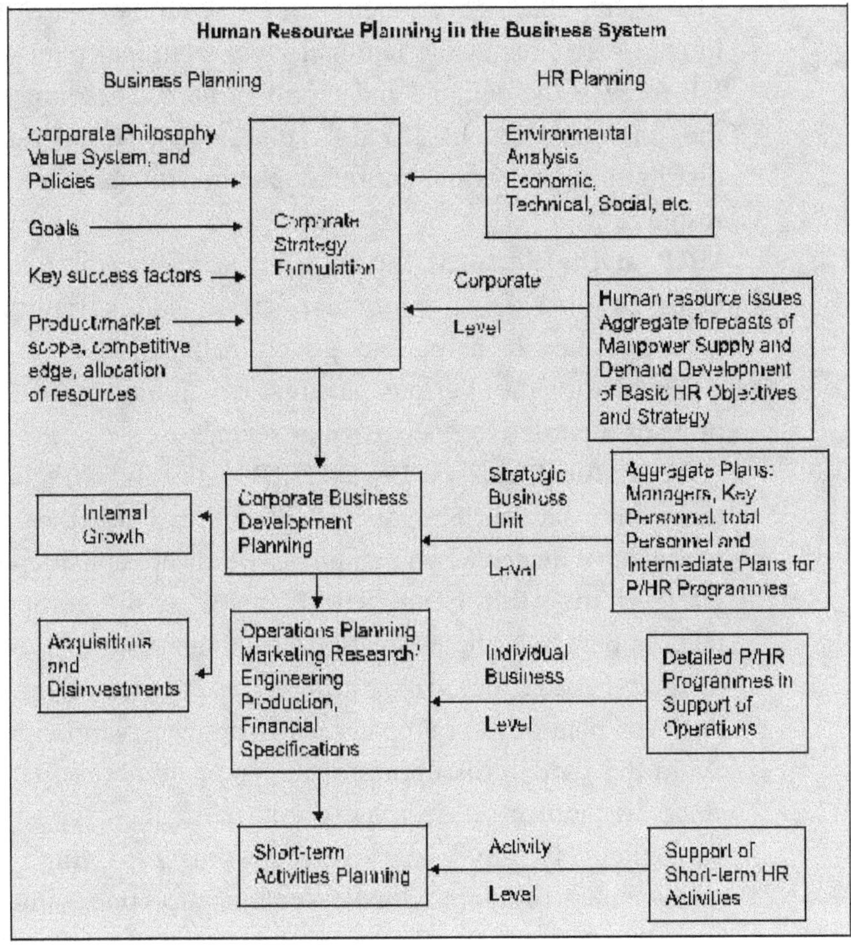

HR PLANNING AT DIFFERENT LEVELS

Human Resource Planning (HRP) may be done at different levels and for different purposes. National planners may make a HR plan at the national level whereas the strategists at a company may make a HR plan at the unit level. The HR Planning thus operates at five levels.

1.   **HRP at National Level:** HRP at the national level helps to plan for educational facilities, health care facilities,

agricultural and industrial development and employment plans, etc. The government of the country plans for human resources at the national level. National plans for HR forecast the demand and supply of human resources at the national level. It also plans for occupational distribution, sectoral and regional allocation of human resources.

2. **HRP at the Sectoral Level**: HRP at the sectoral level helps to plan for a particular sector like agriculture, industry, etc. It helps the government to allocate its resources to the various sectors depending upon the priority accorded to the particular sector.

3. **HRP at the Industry Level**: HRP at the industry level takes into account the output/ operational level of the particular industry when manpower needs are considered.

4. **HRP at the Unit Level**: HR Planning at the company level is based on the estimation of human resource needs of the particular company in question. It is based on the business plan of the company. A manpower plan helps to avoid the sudden disruption of the company's production since it indicates shortages of particular types of personnel, if any, in advance, thus enabling the management to adopt suitable strategies to cope with the situation.

5. **HRP at the Departmental Level**: HRP at the departmental level looks at the manpower needs of a particular department in an organization.

OBJECTIVES OF HUMAN RESOURCE PLANNING

The following are the objectives of human resource planning:

1. Assessing manpower needs for future and making plans for recruitment and selection.

2. Assessing skill requirement in future for the organization.

3. Determining training and the development needs of the organization.

4. Anticipating surplus or shortage of staff and avoiding unnecessary detentions or dismissals.

5. Controlling wage and salary costs.

6. Ensuring optimum use of human resources in the organization.

7. Helping the organization to cope with the technological development and modernization.

8. Ensuring career planning of every employee of the organization and making succession programmes.

9. Ensuring higher labour productivity.

NEED FOR HUMAN RESOURCE PLANNING

Human resource planning is needed for foreseeing the human resource requirements of an organization and supply of human resources. Its need can be assessed from the following points:

1. **Replacement of Persons**: A large number of persons are to be replaced in the organization because of retirement, old age, death, etc. There will be a need to prepare persons for taking up new position in such contingencies.

2. **Labour Turnover**: There is always labour turnover in every organization. The degree of labour turnover may vary from concern to concern but it cannot be eliminated altogether. There will be a need to recruit new persons to take up the positions of those who have left the organization. If the concern is able to forecast turnover rate precisely, then advance efforts are made to recruit and train persons so that work does not suffer for want of workers.

3. **Expansion Plans:** Whenever there is a plan to expand or diversify the concern then more persons will be required to take up new positions. Human resource planning is essential under these situations.

4. **Technological Changes**: The business is working under changing technological environment. There may be a need to give fresh training to personnel. In addition, there may also be a need to infuse fresh blood into the organization. Human resource planning will help in meeting the new demands of the organization.

5. **Assessing Needs**: Human resource planning is also required to determine whether there is any shortage or surplus of persons in the organization. If there are less persons than required, it will adversely affect the work. On the other hand, if more persons are employed than the requirement, then it will increase labour cost, etc. Human resource planning ensures the employment of proper workforce.

Steps in Manpower Planning

Human Resource Planning has to be a systems approach and is carried out in a set procedure. The procedure is as follows:

1. Analysing the current manpower inventory
2. Making future manpower forecasts
3. Developing employment programmes
4. Design training programmes

1. **Analysing the current manpower inventory-** Before a manager makes forecast of future manpower, the current manpower status has to be analysed. For this the following things have to be noted-

    *   Type of organization
    *   Number of departments

- Number and quantity of such departments
- Employees in these work units

Once these factors are registered by a manager, he goes for the future forecasting.

2. **Making future manpower forecasts-** Once the factors affecting the future manpower forecasts are known, planning can be done for the future manpower requirements in several work units.

   The Manpower forecasting techniques commonly employed by the organizations are as follows:

   i. **Expert Forecasts:** This includes informal decisions, formal expert surveys and Delphi technique.

   ii. **Trend Analysis:** Manpower needs can be projected through extrapolation (projecting past trends), indexation (using base year as basis), and statistical analysis (central tendency measure).

   iii. **Work Load Analysis:** It is dependent upon the nature of work load in a department, in a branch or in a division.

   iv. **Work Force Analysis:** Whenever production and time period has to be analysed, due allowances have to be made for getting net manpower requirements.

   v. **Other methods:** Several Mathematical models, with the aid of computers are used to forecast manpower needs, like budget and planning analysis, regression, new venture analysis.

3. **Developing employment programmes-** Once the current inventory is compared with future forecasts, the employment programmes can be framed and developed

accordingly, which will include recruitment, selection procedures and placement plans.

4. **Design training programmes-** These will be based upon extent of diversification, expansion plans, development programmes, etc. Training programmes depend upon the extent of improvement in technology and advancement to take place. It is also done to improve upon the skills, capabilities, knowledge of the workers.

DETERMINANTS OF HRP

There are several factors that affect HRP. These factors or determinants can be classified into external factors and internal factors.

External Factors

- **Government Policies:** Policies of the government like labour policy, industrial relations policy, policy towards reserving certain jobs for different communities and sons-of-the- soils, etc. affect the HRP.
- **Level of Economic Development:** Level of economic development determines the level of HRD in the country and thereby the supply of human resources in future in the country.
- **Business Environment:** External business environmental factors influences the volume and mix of production and thereby the future demand for human resources.
- **Level of Technology:** Level of technology determines the kind of human resources required.
- **International Factors:** International factors like the demand for the resources and supply of human resources in various countries.

Internal Factors

- **Company Policies and Strategies:** Company's policies and strategies relating to expansion diversification, alliances, etc. determines the human resource demand in terms of quality and quantity.

- **Human Resource Policies:** Human resources policies of the company regarding quality of human resource, compensation level, quality of worklife, etc. influences human resource plan.

- **Job Analysis:** Fundamentally, human resource plan is based on job analysis. Job description and job specification determines the kind of employees required.

- **Time Horizons:** Companies with stable competitive environment can plan for the long run whereas the firms with unstable competitive environment can plan for only short-term range.

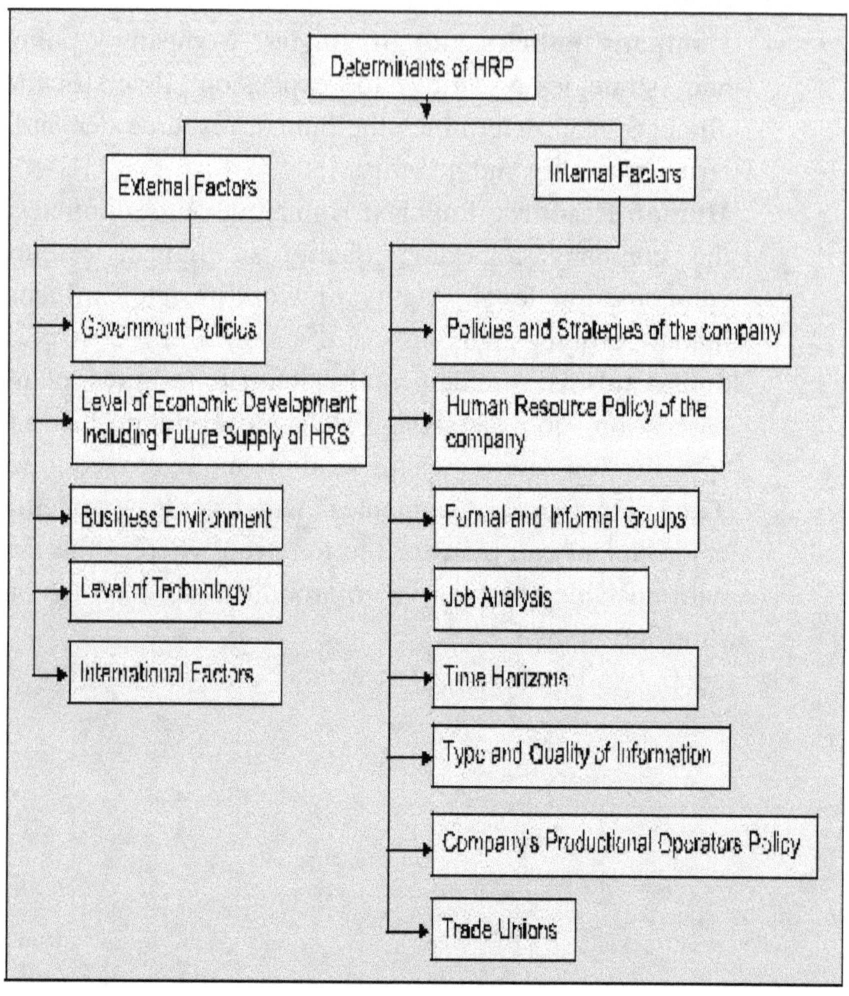

Importance of Manpower Planning

1. **Key to managerial functions-** The four managerial functions, i.e., planning, organizing, directing and controlling are based upon the manpower. Human resources help in the implementation of all these managerial activities. Therefore, staffing becomes a key to all managerial functions.

2. **Efficient utilization-** Efficient management of personnel's becomes an important function in the

industrialization world of today. Setting of large scale enterprises requires management of large scale manpower. It can be effectively done through staffing function.

3. **Motivation-** Staffing function not only includes putting right men on right job, but it also comprises of motivational programmes, i.e., incentive plans to be framed for further participation and employment of employees in a concern. Therefore, all types of incentive plans become an integral part of staffing function.

4. **Better human relations-** A concern can stabilize itself if human relations develop and are strong. Human relations become strong trough effective control, clear communication, effective supervision and leadership in a concern. Staffing function also looks after training and development of the work force which leads to co-operation and better human relations.

5. **Higher productivity-** Productivity level increases when resources are utilized in best possible manner. Higher productivity is a result of minimum wastage of time, money, efforts and energies. This is possible through the staffing and its related activities (Performance appraisal, training and development, remuneration)

Factors Affecting Manpower Planning:

Manpower planning exercise is not an easy tube because it is imposed by various factors such as:

1. It suffers from inaccuracy because it is very difficult to forecast long-range requirements of personnel.

2. Manpower planning depends basically on organisation planning. Overall planning is itself is a difficult task because of changes in economic conditions, which make long term manpower planning difficult.

3. It is difficult to forecast about the personnel with the organisation at a future date. While vacancies caused by retirements can be predicted accurately other factors like resignation, deaths are difficult to forecast.

4. Lack of top management support also frustrates those in charge of manpower planning because in the absence of top management support, the system does not work properly.

5. The problem of forecast becomes more occur in the context of key personnel because their replacement cannot be arranged in short period of time.

Limitations of Human Resource Planning

1. The future is uncertain. There are several external factors viz. Technological, political, cultural, etc. that affects the employment opportunities. Therefore, the management can consider the human resource planning as a guiding factor and cannot rely completely on it.

2. With the surplus manpower, the companies try to remove this imbalance using termination, layoff, and removal of the existing employees. This could create a sense of insecurity among them, and that would result in the loss of their faith in the company.

3. The human resource planning is time-consuming since it collects the complete information regarding the personnel requirements of each department and then finds the suitable sources to satisfy the needs.

4. The human resource planning is an expensive process. All the activities carried out from the time the manpower need arises till the final placement of employees, consumes lot of time and is very expensive.

Thus, the firm must carry out the human resource planning cautiously since it is accorded with several limitations that can adversely affect the overall functioning of the firm.

GUIDELINES FOR MAKING HRP EFFECTIVE

Some of the suggestions for making HR planning effective are as given below:

1. **Integration with Organizational Plans**: Human resource planning must be balanced with organizational plans. It must be based on the organizational objectives and plans. This requires development of good communication channels between organization planners and the human resource planners.

2. **Period of HR Planning**: Period of the planning should be appropriate to the needs and circumstances of the enterprise in question. The size and structure of the enterprise as well as the anticipated changes must be taken into consideration.

3. **Proper Organization:** To be effective, the planning function should be properly organized. If possible, within the human resource department. A separate cell or committee should be constituted to provide adequate focus and to coordinate planning work at various levels.

4. **Support of Top Management:** To be effective in the long run, manpower planning must have the full support of the top management. The support from top management is essential to ensure the necessary resources, cooperation and support for the success of the planning.

5. **Involvement of Operating Executives:** Human resource planning is not a function of manpower planners only. To be effective, it requires active participation and coordinated efforts on the part of operating executives. Such participation will help to improve understanding of the process and thereby reduce resistance.

6. **Efficient and Reliable Information System:** To facilitate human resource planning, an adequate database must be developed for human resources.

7. **Balanced Approach**: The human resource experts should give equal importance to both quantitative and qualitative aspects of manpower. Instead of matching existing people with existing job, stress should be laid on filling future vacancies with right people. Promotion should also be considered carefully. Career planning and development, skill levels, morale, etc. should be given due importance by the planners.

■

Chapter – 4
HUMAN CAPITAL: MEANING AND THEORY

"The most valuable of all capital is that invested in human beings."
Alfred Marshall in *Principles of Economics*

Human capital is the skill, talent, and productivity that employees bring to a company. Coined by University of Chicago economist Theodore Schultz in 1964, the term refers to capital produced by investing in knowledge.

The understanding of human capital has been developing over time. When this concept was first introduced, it was considered disgraceful [**Becker,** 1964/1993]. If any economist suggested that people should be approached in the same manner as capital –being a contributing factor in production –general public regarded this as extremely inappropriate. People saw it in the same way as slavery and dismissed any thought of it. The researcher who coined the term was Theodore Schultz. In his work, **Schultz (1961)** argued that investment in human capital "accounts for most of the impressive rise in the real earnings per worker." Another great contributor in the field was Jacob **Mincer (1958)**, who noticed that the huge dispersion of earnings could be significantly explained by his model of human capital. However, according to the Nobel committee, the most noteworthy contribution to economics in the field of human capital was done by **Gary Becker** [1964/1993]. His view was thathuman capital is directly useful in the production function. In other words, according to Becker, human capital increases worker's productivity in all tasks, though possibly differentially in different tasks, organizations, and situations. The role of human capital in the production process is complex, but it can be represented by a unidimensional object, such as the stock of knowledge or skills. Since 1960s, these economists inspired countless others to follow this line of research and at present there are thousands of studies focusing on various aspects of human capital. One of the most interesting aspects of human capital is that it is embodied in individuals and can therefore not be separated from the individual. Thus, the distribution of human capital rests on one's mobility across locations and firms [Becker 1964/1993].On one hand, this implies that it is extremely rare to loose one's knowledge and skills as opposed to losing their house or financial assets, therefore when someone invests money into his education, it is generally an insured investment.

Today, it is widely acknowledged that human capital is of utmost importance for the economic performance of regions. **Lucas (1988)** and **Romer (1990**) drew attention to this fact in their endogenous growth theory, which proves that countries and regions which exhibit higher levels of human capital should expect higher growth rates than areas with inferior levels.

Human Capital: Definitions

There are many definitions of human capital used in the literature, but most of them stress the economic returns of human capital investment. **Schultz (1961**), for example, defined human capital as "acquired skills and knowledge", to distinguish raw (unskilled) labour from skilled labour. Similarly, the **Penguin Dictionary of Economics (1984)** defined human capital as "the skills, capacities and abilities possessed by an individual which permit him to earn income", a definition which emphasizes the improvement of people's economic situation due to human capital investment. **The World Bank (2006)** similarly defined human capital as the productive capacity embodied in individuals, with special focus on its contribution to economic production.

According to Claudia Goldin- 'Human capital is the stock of productive skills, talents, health and expertise of the labor force, just as physical capital is the stock of plant, equipment, machines, and tools'.

Human capital is **defined in the Oxford English Dictionary** as "the skills the labor force possesses and is regarded as a resource or asset."

Human capital is defined by the **OECD (1998)** as "the knowledge, skills and competences and other attributes embodied in individuals that are relevant to economic activity".

N. Bontis, N. C. Dragonetti, K. Jacobsen a G. Roos (1999) defined the human capital as the human factor in the organization; the combined intelligence, skills and expertise that gives the organization its distinctive character. The human elements of the organization are those that are capable of learning, changing, innovating and providing the creative thrust which if properly motivated can ensure the long-run survival of the organization.

Davenport (1998) says that people possess innate abilities, behaviors and personal energy and these elements make up the human capital they bring to their work.

M. Armstrong (2006) defines the human capital as knowledge and skills which individuals create, maintain, and use.

It encompasses the notion that there are investments in people (e.g., education, training, health) and that these investments increase an individual's productivity. We use the term today as if it were always part of our lingua franca. But it wasn't. Not that long ago, even economists scoffed at the notion of "human capital." As Theodore Schultz noted in his American Economic Association presidential address in 1961 many thought that free people were not to be equated with property and marketable assets (Schultz, 1961). To them, that implied slavery. But the concept of human capital goes back at least to **Adam Smith**. In his fourth definition of capital he noted: "The acquisition of ... talents during ... education, study, or apprenticeship, costs a real expense, which is capital in [a] person. Those talents [are] part of his fortune [and] likewise that of society" **(Smith, 1776).** The earliest formal use of the term "human capital" in economics is probably by Irving Fisher in 1897.It was later adopted by various writers but did not become a serious part of the economists' lingua franca until the late1950s. It became considerably more popular after Jacob Mincer's 1958 Journal of Political Economy article "Investment in Human Capital and Personal Income Distribution." In Gary Becker's Human Capital: A Theoretical and Empirical Analysis, with Special Reference to Education, published in 1964 (and preceded by his 1962 Journal of Political Economy article, "Investment in Human Capital"),Becker notes that he hesitated to use the term "human capital" in the title of his book and employed a long subtitle to guard against

How it works (Example):

Better skills can increase an employee's value in the workplace, and an employer that obtains highly skilled employees can therefore gain a significant competitive advantage via human capital. Human capital is largely responsible for innovation, which can also be a tremendous competitive advantage for companies.

Accordingly, companies are usually very interested in investing in and acquiring human capital. They do this via recruiting new employees, training existing employees, and ensuring that the relationships between employees and their managers are positive.

There are two kinds of human capital: specific and general. Specific human capital refers to knowledge and skills that few find useful and are willing to pay for. For example, knowing how to operate a proprietary machine that is owned and operated by Company XYZ might be a skill that only Company XYZ is willing to pay for. General human capital refers to knowledge and skills that many employers find useful, such as knowing accounting, knowing how to transplant a heart, or knowing how to design a bridge.

Why it Matters:

Employment is essentially the purchase and sale of human capital: employees own their talents, skills, and time, and they sell these assets to companies in return for money. This is the idea underlying the philosophy that employees are really consultants who sell their time and expertise to clients, and that the value of one's labor is not always based on his or her amount of physical exertion but on the market value of his or her knowledge and skills. Some economists argue that market rates are not the only thing that establishes the value of skills and knowledge; personal connections, prestigious schooling, and character can also influence the value of one's human capital.

Human capital tends to migrate in global economies, most often from poor places to richer places. Some economists argue that this "brain drain" makes poor places poorer and rich places richer.

DETERMINANTS OF HUMAN CAPITAL

Specialisation and division of labour: Specialisation allows workers to concentrate on specific tasks and increased specialisation of skills.

"The greatest improvement in the productive powers of labour.. seem to have been the effects of the division of labour."

– Adam Smith

Education: Basic education to improve literacy and numeracy has an important implication for a basis of human capital.

Vocational training: Direct training for skills related to jobs, electrician, plumbing nursing. A skilled profession requires particular vocational training.

A climate of creativity: An education which enables children to think outside the box can increase human capital in a way that 'rote learning' and an impressive accumulation of facts may not.

Infrastructure: The infrastructure of an economy will influence human capital. Good transport, communication, availability of mobile phones and the internet are very important for the development of human capital in developing economies.

Competitiveness: An economy dominated by state monopolies is likely to curtail individual creativity and entrepreneurs. An environment which encourages self-employment and the creation of business enables greater use of potential human capital in an economy.

Importance of human capital

Structural unemployment: Individuals whose human capital is inappropriate for modern employers may struggle to gain employment. A major issue in modern economies is that rapid deindustrialisation has left many manual workers, struggling to thrive in a very different labour market.

Quality of employment: In the modern economy, there is increasing divergence between low-skilled, low-paid temporary jobs (gig economy). High-skilled and creative workers have increased opportunities for self-employment or good employment contracts.

Economic growth and productivity: Long-term economic growth depends increasingly on improvements in human capital. Better educated, innovative and creative workforce can help increase labour productivity and economic growth.

Human capital flight: An era of globalisation and greater movement of workers has enabled skilled workers to move from low-income countries to higher income countries. This can have adverse effects for developing economies who lose their best human capital.

Limited raw materials: Economic growth in countries with limited natural resources, e.g. Japan, Taiwan and South East Asia. Rely on high-skilled, innovative workforce adding value to raw materials in the manufacturing process.

Sustainability: "what we leave to future generations; whether we leave enough resources, of all kinds, to provide them with the opportunities at least as large as the ones we have had ourselves" (UN, 2012)

METHODS TO MEASURE HUMAN CAPITAL

There are several viewpoints vis-à-vis the meaning of human capital. Different points of views almost always lead to incongruent measures. There are two strands which are indicators or non-monetary respect and monetary one. The indicator-based may be either qualitative or quantitative. The quantity might take the form of average years of schooling, educational attainment levels whereas the quality might be assessed by standardized or unstandardized test scores - overall combined or a specific section - class size and the ratio of student per teacher, for instance. The other strand, in contrast, is in the form of monetary term since human capital measures might be either direct or indirect estimates. The indirect estimates are derived from what can be inferred or the residual approach while direct estimates, resulted from direct estimations based on various components. The direct estimates can be divided into two major methods, the cost-based and the income-based approaches. These methods are standard and frequently used since if we consider human capital as a form of investment, then it is typical to think of its cost and returns, measured by income obtained from such investment. This regard has been backed up by theories and studies, so that the approaches for human capital measurement are provided as follows:

The Cost-Based Approach

This method was first introduced by Ernst Engel in 1883 and assumes that an individual's monetary value coincides with his production cost. Engel determined man's value on the basis of the costs incurred for rearing a child. The measurement unit chosen was the economic cost from birth to a certain age. The basic principle underlying the whole model is that an individual's value (human capital) tends to equal their production costs, i.e. the expenses incurred to maintain individuals from the moment of their birth.

This approach originally measures human capital by viewing it as the cost of production. However, this method is frequently referred to the sum of the depreciated value of past investment undertaken by individuals, households, firms, organizations, and governments, so sometimes it is called "backward-looking" approach. It also encompasses all of costs or expenses incurred as human capital has been producing such as the opportunity cost associated with attending school. Not only does this method include monetary outlays by the agents previously mentioned, but also take in non-market inputs such as time spent to education by students and other related persons. The cost-based measure is simple enough to measure when dealing with both private and public expenditures on education at aggregative level. Similarly, this method can legitimately incorporate the expenses of adult training, health, safety, as well as the values of in rearing and mobility. This is so because they are part of such costs of investment in human capital, too.

According to the structure of this cost-based approach, the flows of resources used for the purposes of human capital investment in education and other related parts can be measured. As a consequence, this approach is consistent with the income-based approach since one can easily envision it as the cost-benefit analysis, which is widely used when it nails down to investment.

Pros and Cons:

One of the flaws pertaining to this method is that it should not be taken as an estimation of human capital since it is just a summation of historical costs and ignores the social costs that are invested in people. This means that if we aim to measure it more accurately, the stock of human capital by the cost-based approach should be separated into tangible and intangible. The tangible part consists of the costs required to produce the physical human being. In contrast, the intangible investment should aim at enhancing the quality or productivity of workers. They should include expenditures on health, mobility, education and training, and the opportunity costs of students attending school. This will provide an estimate of the resources invested in the education and other human capital respects, which can be useful for cost-benefit analyses. The bright side, though, it is quite easy to apply, owing to the ready availability of data both on public and private spending. Nevertheless, as is well known with physical capital, there is no relationship guarantee between investments and the quality of output. The value of capital is determined by the demand for it, not by the cost of production. This problem tends to be more serious with human capital per se.

The weakest aspect of this method consists in the fact that it does not estimate human capital but only provides an evaluation of the costs required to form that individual. The retrospective method suggests measuring human capital like physical capital evaluating the total amount of resources invested into a child's rearing from the time of their birth.

The Income-Based Approach

This method was labelled by Marshall as "income capitalization approach" and consists in an estimate of the actual value of a worker's probable future earnings after deducting expenses. The probabilities of premature death and unemployment in the course of a worker's life are also accounted for. As indicated by its name this approach refers to a present estimate of future earnings.

The first person who tried to provide an explicit estimate of an individual's value was Sir

W. Petty (Petty, 1690) at the end of the 17th century. Petty was driven by fiscal motivations connected to accounting issues in England. In order to estimate the economic value of the working population Petty established each worker's value on the basis of labour-generated income and came to the conclusion that this income corresponds to the yield of the human capital generating it capitalized in perpetuity at a certain interest rate.

Petty calculated human capital's monetary value in order to estimate a country's contribution capacity and this prompted his assertion that human capital plays a key role in a nation's wealth. In his estimates of the human capital of England Petty included the annual national wage, the average time period needed to attain it and the market interest rate for a capitalization of its value over time.

This approach measures human capital by summing the discounted values of all future income streams that all individuals expect to earn throughout their working life or lifetime. Since this method is essentially the total expected returns on investment after the time deductions and they start to pay off when one begins working, sometimes it is called "forward-looking" approach. This forward-looking approach attempts to evaluate one's earnings profile, so that human capital valued is appraised at the market prices. This is because the labor market deems workers many factors, including abilities, efforts, education, and the institutional and technological structures of the economy.

According to this method, there are some underlying assumptions worth mentioning. First, it is taken for granted that people invest in human capital just once in their life time.

Second, the returns to investment would incur after one stops investing, before that and after the retirement age, such the returns are presumably zero. And international trade does not exist in this model. In brief, in this *method* a human being is regarded as an item of fixed capital. Each individual generates wealth in their job. Thus, the combination of intellectual, physical and mental abilities of each single individual represents an economic asset (human capital). Any action directed to improving such a combination of abilities represents a real investment which enhances the value and quality of future production.

Pros and Cons:

One salient characteristic of this income approach is that it is forward-looking. Thereby, a dynamic economy that aims at measuring its income capacities would clearly get more benefit than the backward-looking cost approach. Nevertheless, this approach suffers from its consistency with the real world. For example, the model assumes that differences in wages can perfectly reflect differences in productivity. In reality, wages do vary, so income-based measures of human capital will be biased. Also, these measures are subject to the discount rate and the retirement age. Whether maintenance costs should be deducted is another drawback. There are controversies over this issue. Some scholars point out that this income approach has a serious problem due to not deducting maintenance costs from gross earnings, so some others attempt to account for this but still face difficulties. For instance, what kind of expenditure should be classified as maintenance, and how to account for economies of scale and 'public' goods when estimating per capita consumption for different members in the same household? Another weak point lies in that data on earnings are not as widely available as data on investment. This is especially true for developing countries, where the wage rate is often not adequately observable or even unreliable. However, a number of people flavors this approach because it simple to measure and it represents the notion that if if one has more human capital, he or she should earn more as well over the course of the lifetime.

The Output-Based Approach

This approach measures human capital by its output. In other words, several indicators that can sufficiently represent the stock of human capital as a whole or at least as a group might be employed as the proxy. It is important to note that this approach does not directly view human capital as accumulated. Rather, it tends to find a suitable indicator or index that reflects the amount of human capital of an economy or a group of people. They might be average years of schooling, literacy rate, enrolment rate, net enrolment, gross enrolment, or some other educational attainment indexes. Because of its variegated indicators, average years of schooling which is one of the most popular and easy-to-measure proxies for human capital following this output approach stand out.

Pros and Cons:

Like other approaches, this output-based measure has a number of drawbacks. Firstly, if the school enrolment is used as the proxy, it would be problematic since the school enrolment is the flow but human capital is a stock per se. Secondly, when dealing with international data, the gross enrolment is used rather than the net because of conformity and availability. This would lead to an econometric issue called "measurement error." Nevertheless, its advantage includes the data availability, simple calculation, and easy interpretation and understanding

The main contributions which have tried to evaluate human capital quantitatively and provide a measurement for the otherwise vague economic notion of human capital will be illustrated in this section. Most studies aimed at human capital measurement (an individual's monetary value) can be classified according to two different methods: a *retrospective method* and a *prospective method*. This dichotomy reflects the twofold measurement approach adopted to estimate individual monetary value. In the former method reference is made to individuals as consumers. Individuals are valued as the amount of the resources spent for their maintenance and training. In the latter method reference is made to individuals as producers. Individuals are valued by means of the income which they generate. The *retrospective method* is a cost-based method which estimates human capital as the costs incurred for producing individuals from their birth to the time when they enter the labour market. The *prospective method* is an income-based approach which values human capital by estimating an individual's future earnings.

HUMAN CAPITAL THEORY
Basic Premise of Theory

Human Capital Theory refers to the aggregate stock of competencies, knowledge, social, and personal attributes embodied in the ability to create intrinsic and measurable economic value. Human Capital Theory views humans and individuals as economic units acting as their own economy. The role of human capital is widely discussed in economic development, productivity analysis, innovation, public policy, and education.

Basic Concepts, Relationships between Concepts and Assumptions

The basic concept of Human Capital Theory is that investments in individuals can be mathematically measured based on the economic value they are able to contribute to society.

Human capital is often subdivided into categories such as cultural capital, social capital, economic capital, and symbolic capital. Human capital is developed in many ways. Economic capital is typically measured by the ability to perform labor which results in economic value. Education, job training, and marketable talents are all ways in which humans increase their ability to acquire knowledge and generate higher wages. Social capital and cultural capital refer to the relationships and influence individuals contribute to society. Although social, cultural, and symbolic capital are very difficult to measure, understanding their existence and value is still vital. Each type of human capital is important and the combination of all types generate total human capital.

The assumptions of human capital theory revolve around the immeasurable nature of its many forms. Economic capital can be measured by its ability to produce wages, however, an intrinsic value of human capital exists although it is not always measurable. Secondly, human capital may be stored but not fully utilized at all times therefore making it difficult to observe and study consistently.

Evaluation of the Theory

Human capital theory is relatively consistent across different disciplines; the different types of human capital are more relevant depending on the primary subject matter. Measuring economic human capital and its return on investment is a vital aspect of the proposed theory. The measurement of human capital is done in many ways and new metrics are being developed to measure traditionally difficult fields such as social capital (Klout score).

Human capital theory has practical implication for determining the value of training and education. It allows individuals to calculate the expected future returns of an investment in education. In addition, human capital theory's utility allows individuals to quantify the value of their intangible assets such as education and social status.

Applications

The theory of human capital has both planning utility and measurement utility. Consumer economics and financial planning often measures the value of current choices versus their long run returns and implications. Human Capital Theory allows individuals to make decisions about the inherent cost of future opportunities weighted with the opportunity cost of present situations. Human capital theory also introduces the investment risks of human capital theory including its illiquidity and assumptions about payback periods and opportunity cost. Again, human capital theory can be applied to the lives of graduate students when looking at time allocation and the investments in health and social capital. Investments in both physical health and mental health are both necessary to maximizing overall human capital. Finally, measuring the intrinsic value of a PhD allows graduate students to continue their course of action even if the economic returns and opportunity cost produce a negative monetary return.

Schultz's Theory of Human Capital

Theodore W. Schultz publishes an article in the ***American Economic Review*** (1961) entitled **"Investment in Human Capital."** In this article, Schultz introduces his theory of Human Capital. He argues that both knowledge and skill are a form of capital, and that this capital is a product of "deliberate investment." Schultz highlights Western countries, and explains their increase in national output as a result of investment in human capital. He also makes a direct link between an increase in investment in human capital, and the overall increase in workers earnings.

He argues that economists have been afraid to relate to human beings as capital. Schultz believes that the concept of human capital has negative connotations that arise from the American experience of slavery, and that society is hypersensitive towards anything that serves as a reminder of that system. For Schultz, however, **the concept of human capital implies an investment in people**. He argues that education, training, and investments in health open up opportunities and choices that otherwise would be unavailable to many individuals. Schultz compares the acquisition of knowledge and skills to acquiring the "means of production." Workers no longer have to be at the mercy of others; instead they can be in control of increasing their own productivity and earnings. Schultz argues that the difference in earnings between people relates to the differences in access to education and health. For example, when farm folk move to the city, or when African-American kids look to find work, they experience a barrier that arises from their lack of human capital (i.e., appropriate knowledge and skill). Schultz also argues that in many underdeveloped countries, food and shelter are of primary concern, and thus there are short-term investments made to deal with these crises. In societies whose main concern is not basic needs, there is the opportunity for long-term investment in education, health, and migration (i.e., helping people adjust by finding them jobs and offering them the opportunity to learn/improve their skills). In the long-term these investments will strengthen the economy and raise the standard of living.

Schultz argues that investment in human capital must focus on supporting individuals in acquiring an education, since it is skill and knowledge that affect one's ability to do productive work. He believes that an investment to enhance these capabilities leads to an increase in human productivity, which in turn leads to a positive rate of return. Schultz criticizes those who see investment in human capital as a cost. He argues that while in the short-term there may be a cost (i.e., cost of facility, loss of earnings for workers while in school, etc), in the long-term the yield from the investment will far outweigh the cost.

Criticism of Schultz's Theory

Since this theory first appeared, there has been much praise (in 1979 Schultz received the Nobel Prize in Economic Sciences) and much criticism for human capital theory. Today, many still believe that society needs to invest in people for the sake of a stronger, more productive economy, and also to increase the opportunities and choices open to the individual. At the same time, however, many criticize the Human Capital Theory as serving the needs of those in power (i.e., government and business), and not the individual.

Paul Bouchard, in his article entitled **"Training and Work; Myths about Human Capital"** challenges seven basic assumptions contained in Schultz' theory. Briefly, they are as follows:

Assumption 1: Human Capital is in investment in the future.

-It is impossible to accurately predict future labour market needs. All the forecasting tools we have are problematic. **Assumption 2**: More training leads to better work skills.

-Organizations value particular skills and what these are often change over time. There are not necessarily 'better' skills, just ones that fit what serve the needs of the organization at the time.

Assumption 3: Educational institutions play a central role in the development of human capital.

-Today our traditional educational institutions are not as relevant or effective as they could be. Things change so fast that people tend to learn more on the job.

Assumption 4: Employees need to improve their skills. -Work has not become more complex, in fact, with technology things have become 'easier'. The need to improve one's skills comes from having to compete in a job market with people who are in many cases over-qualified.

Assumption 5: Training enhances employability. -Many individuals do not have access to training and thus access to jobs, while others may have access to training, but not to mobility within the organization.

Assumption 6: Training can compensate for skill shortages. -Bouchard argues there are not skill shortages, rather there is a skill-mismatch. In other words, for various reasons, individuals with appropriate skills do not find work. Three potential reasons for this are: labour market dynamics, structural discrimination, and employee self-selection.

Assumption 7: Employment and unemployment are economic concepts. -The labour market is NOT a market like any other. There are social forces present that keep people from having equal access to employment regardless of their skill and experience.

A major issue with Schultz' theory is that it places the onus on the individual for becoming 'educated', finding employment, and becoming a productive member of society. The theory implies that if an individual does not succeed it is their fault (i.e., they are too lazy, not bright enough, etc.), as opposed to a bias in the system. This is a tremendous burden because for many their inability to find work is due to factors beyond their control (i.e., socio-economic status, ethnicity, gender, etc), and not necessarily to their unwillingness or inability. Finally, knowledge and skill gained through education is not necessarily what is important to employers. As **Bowles and Gintis (1976)** and many others have pointed out, the characteristics that an individual who has been through the formal educational system possesses (i.e., obedience, responsibility, etc), are in many cases more attractive to employers than their knowledge and skill.

■

CHAPTER – 5
ECONOMICS OF EDUCATION

From a **theoretical** perspective, education can be viewed as an investment into the knowledge and skills of people. It equips people with the skills that make them more productive in performing their work tasks and it conveys the knowledge and competencies that enable people to generate and adopt the new ideas that spur innovation and technological progress. To the extent that this increases individual productivity, educated *individuals* will be able to earn higher wages and – in societies with effective minimum wages – less likely to be unemployed. At the *macroeconomic* level, education can spur long-run economic growth by increasing aggregate productivity through accumulated human capital and by helping to generate and diffuse innovations which bring technological progess. Beyond the economic benefits in the narrow sense, education also offers nonproduction benefits such as increased work satisfaction, improved health decisions, reduced crime, improved citizenship, and better parenting.

Education can serve many goals. It can empower people to be independent citizens and participate in society. It can promote civic awareness and foster a shared system of values and social cohesion. It can increase health consciousness and prevent criminal behavior. It can also serve mere "consumption" purposes: the pure joy of increasing our understanding of the world. The case for education can thus be made from many perspectives.

Education and Productivity

The fundamental insight of human capital theory is that education can be viewed as an **investment** into the knowledge and skills of people. Similar to investments in machinery, those who invest in their education incur an initial cost in the hope to reap benefits in the future. The costs in this investment decision include both direct costs such as educational material and tuition fees and the opportunity cost that the people could use their time for other activities such as working for income. As pointed out in the introduction, the benefits can take many forms, but in a pure economic perspective, the main expected return is the increased **productivity** that comes along with higher knowledge and skills: Education equips people with the skills that make them more productive in performing their work tasks and it conveys the knowledge and competencies that enable people to generate and adopt the new ideas that spur innovation and technological progress.

If a more educated person contributes a larger marginal product to the production process of a firm, in a market economy the firm will pay the person higher **earnings** accordingly. To the extent that the increases in future income streams are valued higher than the initial costs, the investment in education will be viewed as worthwhile from an economic perspective. This basic insight goes as far back as to Adam Smith (1776) who wrote in his Wealth of Nations-

"A man educated at the expense of much labour and time to any of those employments which require extraordinary dexterity and skill, may be compared to an expensive machine. The work which he learns to perform, it must be expected, over and above the usual wages of common labour, will replace to him the whole expense of his education, with at least the ordinary profits of an equally valuable capital."

Education may enable people to escape unemployment and find a job in the first place. In addition, education may increase individuals' ability to deal with changing conditions, thereby enhancing employability in times of rapid technological changes. By reducing unemployment and increasing earnings, investing in people's education and skills can thus ultimately help to avoid poverty, reduce social exclusion, and reduce inequality in society.

The productivity-enhancing features of education almost certainly contain increased **cognitive skills**, both at a general and at an occupation-specific level, that enable people to better understand, perform, and improve economic processes. In addition, education may also affect **non-cognitive skills** and personality traits that have an economic payoff.

Most importantly, available evidence suggests that in reality educational processes will tend to further several productivity-relevant skills at the same time, rather than enhancing one skill dimension at the detriment of another. Beyond the benefits in terms of increased productivity that is remunerated on the labor market, education may also offer a range of **nonproduction benefits**. These may include such aspects as increased work satisfaction, improved decision-making on health issues, reduced crime, improved citizenship, and better parenting. Some of these nonproduction benefits may accrue at the individual level, whereas others may accrue to society at large.

Data also support this fact that earnings of educated people is higher than the uneducated. According to information released by the U.S. Census Bureau in February 2012, workers with a college degree earn nearly twice as much as those without one in 2009. Census data indicates that the earnings of the average worker between the ages of 25 and 34 with a high school diploma was $27,511. The average earnings of a similar worker armed with a bachelor's degree was $45,692. Taking these earnings into account, spread over the course of a 40-year career and not accounting for inflation and salary increases, results in roughly $1.1 million for the high school graduate and $1.8 million for the college graduate (Smith Lisa, 2014).

Look Beyond the Money

The significant earnings that a college graduate can expect provide the opportunity to enjoy material comforts. A nice car, a nice home and some spending money in your pocket are the traditional rewards for financial success. Likewise, increased earnings provide an opportunity to save and invest. College graduates have the opportunity to not to only enjoy a comfortable lifestyle during their working years, but their increased earnings provide an opportunity to save and invest to ensure a financially secure retirement.

While there's no doubt the pay checks are nice, attending college has additional financial and intangible benefits too. A number of studies suggest that higher education leads to better health consciousness, which translates into time spent at the gym or engaging in other forms of exercise. Healthier eating habits often go hand-in-hand with a good exercise regimen, and exercise and healthy eating habits lead to healthier lifestyles, overall.

A college education also provides greater opportunities for promotion and upward social mobility, not only for the recipient of the degree but for non-working spouses and children, as well. An increase in job security and a decrease in unemployment are also associated with a college education, as college graduates tend to have transferable skills. Therefore, if the widget factory closes down, a college-educated accountant or human resources professional can often transfer their skills to another employer with relative ease.

Education and Macroeconomic Development

Apart from its impact at the individual level, education has also entered theories of economic **growth** at the macroeconomic level. There are two broad classes of theoretical models on the specific mechanisms by which education may affect the long-run development of the economy. The first class of models builds directly on the microeconomic theory of human capital described above. The output of the macro economy is simply a function of capital and labor as factors of production. If education works as an investment that increases individual productivity, human capital is a factor of production also in the macro economy that can be accumulated. The increased individual productivity simply aggregates at the economy level. On the transition path from the old steady state of economic output to the new higher steady state, the growth rate of the economy will increase. In such so-called augmented neoclassical growth models, education simply lifts **macroeconomic productivity** by accumulating human capital.

The second class of models highlights the role of education in generating and diffusing new technologies. Ultimately, an economy's rate of growth depends on technological progress, or improvements in the technology that transforms factors of production into output. Such improvements in total factor productivity emerge from **innovation** of products and processes. In so-called endogenous growth models, innovation arises from intentional investments in research and development. This process is fundamentally guided by the underlying invention of people, which flows from the knowledge and skills of the population. Here, education plays the crucial role of increasing the innovative capacity of the economy by producing a continuing stream of new ideas and technologies. By inventing and marketizing these new ideas and new technologies, highly educated people give rise to sustained growth dynamics in these models.

Relatedly, in technological **diffusion** models, the rate at which economies can absorb the technological developments that happen outside depends again on the knowledge and skills of its population. These macroeconomic effects of education stem from increased productivity and income within a country.

Higher levels of education in a country allow it to innovate, to improve its production, and to import and employ new technologies without decreasing the growth prospects for other countries. What is more, a country's education may generate positive spillovers if, by pushing out the world technological frontier, it allows other countries to profit by imitation and reaching a higher productivity level.

Theoretically, the macroeconomic (social) returns to education may be higher or lower than the individual (private) returns discussed above. On the one hand, the macro returns may exceed the individual returns if there are **externalities**. For example, in the spirit of the innovation effects emphasized in endogenous growth models, high-skilled inventors may produce innovations that also raise the productivity of other workers and ultimately of whole economies without all these benefits accruing to the innovator.14 On the other hand, the social returns to education may also be lower than the private returns if part of the private returns comes in the form of unproductive **signaling** or screening.15 Individuals may get more education simply to signal high ability to the labor market, so that educational institutions simply act as devices to select more able students as opposed to providing them with new knowledge and skills.

Economics of Education

The significance of education and human capital has been brought out in many studies and arguments of economic growth and development. This can be classified into the micro and macro levels.

Micro level

At the micro level, the theory postulates that an individual bears the costs (direct costs such as fees paid and indirect costs such as opportunity cost on student time) of education because s/he expect that this investment will create a future stream of benefits to h/her (higher productivity and thus higher wages). There's a significant bulk of literature and research to underscore this fact: For instance, Psacharopoulos and Patrinos study *"Human capital and rates of return"* (2004) conclude that educational quality, (measured by cognitive skills) has a strong impact on individual earnings, moreover educational quality has a strong and robust influence on economic growth with "truly causal relationships". McIntosh and Vignoles (2001) studied wages in the United Kingdom and found strong returns to this investment while Finnie and Meng (2002) and Green and Riddell (2003) established the same fact in Canada. Nickell (2004) considered how differences in the distribution of incomes across countries were affected by the distribution of skill and concluded that "the bulk of the variation in earnings dispersion was generated by skill dispersion. Other studies have also concluded that skills have an increasing impact on the distribution of income and that the income distribution becomes more dispersed in reflection of growing rewards to individual skills (Juhn, Murphy and Pierce 1993, Levy and Murnane (1992). Psacharopoulos (2004) concludes more schooling is associated with higher individual earnings.

Basically, the higher the education level, the higher the income. For example, people with professional degrees earned 6x as much as people who did not graduate from high school (in 2009: $128,000 vs. $20,000). Therefore, more "educated" people tend to earn higher wages and have better jobs than the less "educated" ones (UNDP, 2010)

However, education is not just an income effect. Table 2 demonstrates that unemployment rates and educational attainment are also strongly related.

In other words, the better educated the group, the lower the unemployment rate i.e. at the extremes, unemployment rate for those with less than a high school education was 7%, and the highest reaching 15%, a four-year college degree and at least some graduate school had unemployment rates of 4.5%, compared to an overall rate of 9%.

Also according to the theory, other benefits of education may be realised in terms of greater productivity and less need to incur costs. An example of educational benefit that improves production possibilities is the greater labour market productivity of those with additional schooling. And the lesser dependency on subsidies in educated communities is an example of benefit that reduces costs for tax-payers (Vila, 2000). In addition, a large body of literature in macroeconomics has underscored that productivity spillovers are important determinants of economic growth and that an increase in aggregate human capital will have an effect on aggregate productivity[3] which is as a results of an increase in an individual's education on productivity (Moretti, 2005).

Theory predicts that increases in the overall level of education can benefit society in ways that are not fully reflected in the *private returns* of educated workers, what is otherwise referred to as the 'externalities of education'. For instance, social groups, communities or countries where the average schooling is higher offer, as a rule, better living conditions, both material and non-material, than those where the population is less educated (Vila, 2000).

Macro level

At the macro level, Robert (1991) developed a human capital model which shows that education and the creation of human capital is responsible for both the differences in labour productivity and the differences in overall levels of technology that we observe in the world today. This, according to him, explains the spectacular growth in East Asia that has given education and human capital their current popularity in the field of economic growth and development. Countries such as Hong Kong, Korea, Singapore, and Taiwan have achieved unprecedented rates of economic growth while making large investments in education. This correlation between education, national and international development can be traced to the Solow growth model, way back in the mid-1950s. This theoretical model asserts that the economic growth of a country depends on its endowments of labour (population size) and of physical capital (machinery, infrastructure), and on technological change. In 1962, Edward Denison used the Solow growth accounting framework to examine the factors that contributed to economic growth in the US over the period 1910 to 1960. Denison established that increases in the quantity of labour and of physical capital during that period did not explain the increase in national income and the huge unexplained growth residual but concluded that as much as 23% of the annual growth rate of GNP could be explained by increases in the level of education of the workforce. In other words, education was an important determinant of economic growth. Much later, Denison (1985) found that the increase in schooling of the average worker between 1929 and 1982 explained about one fourth of the rise in per capita income during this period. Even in African countries such as Kenya, education contributed to much to economic development, particularly in the phase up to the mid-1970s during which the economy grew at a comparable rate to the economies of East Asia and when agricultural improvements benefited from educational advance (Green A. et.al, 2007). But detailed investigations on rates of return from education to families and national economies were undertaken by George Psacharopoulos in the 1970s and 1980s who like those before him, concluded that indeed education played a significant role in the social-economic development of a country.

ECONOMICS OF EDUCATION – THE SCHOOLING MODEL

The basic assumption (i.e. maximisation of the PV of lifetime earnings) is quite strong. Education & training are valued only because they increase earnings. Present value (PV) allows comparison of money amounts spent and received in different time periods.

$$PV = y/(1+r)t$$

(PV is the present value of y money received t years from now, - r is the discount rate.)

- Non-monetary rewards of 'schooling' are neglected for simplicity. But there are many of these.

A simple model:

- 18 year old who finished high-school: To go or not to go to university for four years?
- Assume for simplicity there is no on-the-job training if s/he joins the workforce instead of going to university. Also, assume skills learned at school do not depreciate over time. In that case, the person's productivity does not change after leaving school and his/her real income stays approx. constant over the life-cycle.

Picture 5.1

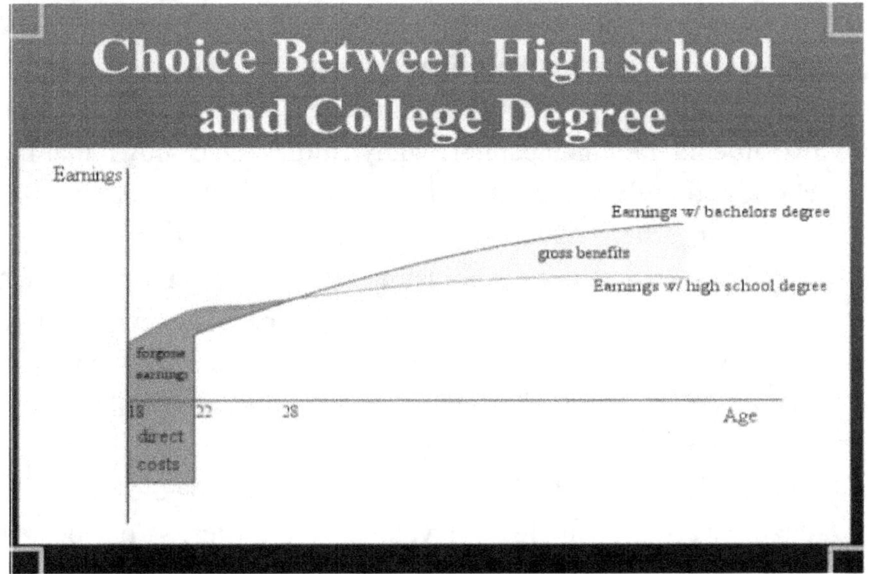

WCOL has to be greater than **WHS** or no person would go to university (the higher wage is like a compensating differential for the higher training costs).

Go to College if PVCOL > PVHS

GARY S. BACKER'S THEORY

To most people capital means a bank account, a hundred shares of IBM stock, assembly lines, or steel plants in the Chicago area. These are all forms of capital in the sense that they are assets that yield income and other useful outputs over long periods of time.

But these tangible forms of capital are not the only ones. Schooling, a computer training course, expenditures of medical care, and lectures on the virtues of punctuality and honesty also are capital. That is because they raise earnings, improve health, or add to a person's good habits over much of his lifetime. Therefore, economists regard expenditures on education, training, medical care, and so on as investments in human capital. They are called human capital because people cannot be separated from their knowledge, skills, health, or values in the way they can be separated from their financial and physical assets.

Education and training are the most important investments in human capital. Many studies have shown that high school and college education in the United States greatly raise a person's income, even after netting out direct and indirect costs of schooling, and even after adjusting for the fact that people with more education tend to have higher IQs and better-educated and richer parents. Similar evidence is now available for many years from over a hundred countries with different cultures and economic systems. The earnings of more educated people are almost always well above average, although the gains are generally larger in less developed countries. Consider the differences in average earnings between college and high school graduates in the United States during the past fifty years. Until the early sixties college graduates earned about 45 percent more than high school graduates. In the sixties this premium from college education shot up to almost 60 percent, but it fell back in the seventies to under 50 percent. The fall during the seventies led some economists and the media to worry about "overeducated Americans." Indeed, in 1976 Harvard economist Richard Freeman wrote a book titled The Overeducated American. This sharp fall in the return to investments in human capital put the concept of human capital itself into some disrepute. Among other things it caused doubt about whether education and training really do raise productivity or simply provides signals ("credentials") about talents and abilities.

But the monetary gains from a college education rose sharply again during the eighties, to the highest level in the past fifty years. Economist Kevin M. Murphy and Finis Welch have shown that the premium on getting a college education in the eighties was over 65 percent. Lawyers, accountants, engineers, and many other professionals experienced especially rapid advances in earnings. The earnings advantage of high school graduates over high school dropouts has also greatly increased. Talk about overeducated Americans has vanished, and it has been replaced by concern once more about whether the United States provides adequate quality and quantity of education and other training.

Gary S. Becker (1962) has provided a general analysis of investment in human capital.

It eventually became apparent that this general analysis would do much more than fill a gap in formal economic theory: it offers a unified explanation of a wide range of empirical phenomena which have either been given, ad hoc interpretations or have baffled investigators.

Among these phenomena are the following:

(1)   Earnings typically increase with age at a decreasing rate. Both the rate of increase and the rate of retardation tend to be positively related to the level of skill.

(2)   Unemployment rates tend to be inversely related to the level of skill.

(3)   Firms in underdeveloped countries appear to be more "paternalistic" toward employees than those in developed countries.

(4)   Younger persons change jobs more frequently and receive more schooling and on-the-job training than older persons do.

(5)   The distribution of earnings is positively skewed, especially among professional and other skilled workers.

(6)   Abler persons receive more education and other kinds of training than others.

(7)   The division of labor is limited by the extent of the market.

(8)   The typical investor in human capital is more impetuous and thus more likely to err than is the typical investor in tangible capital.

Gary S. Becker produced the above said ad hoc arguments in general form, with the emphasis placed on empirical implications.

Becker's key components of Human Capital are investment in **on-the-job training, schooling, information and health.**

A brief discussion of these concepts is as follows:

1   ON-THE-JOB TRAINING

Many workers increase their productivity by learning new skills and perfecting old ones while on the job. Presumably, future productivity can be improved only at a cost, for otherwise there would be an unlimited demand for training. Included in cost are the value placed on the time and effort of trainees, the "teaching" provided by others, and the equipment and materials used. These are costs in the sense that they could have been used in producing current output if they had not been used in raising future output. The amount spent and the duration of the training period depend partly on the type of training since more is spent for a longer time on, say, an intern than a machine operator.

Consider explicitly now a firm that is hiring employees for a specified time period (in the limiting case this period approaches zero), and for the moment assume that both labor and product markets are perfectly competitive. If there were no on-the-job training, wage rates would be given to the firm and would be independent of its actions.

A profit-maximizing firm would be in equilibrium when marginal products equaled wages, that is, when marginal receipts equaled marginal expenditure. Training might lower current receipts and raise current expenditures, yet firms could profitably provide this training if future receipts were sufficiently raised or future expenditures sufficiently lowered

(I)   General Training

General training is useful in many firms besides those providing it; for example, a machinist trained in the army finds his skills of value in steel and aircraft firms, and a doctor trained (interned) at one hospital finds his skills useful at other hospitals. Most on-the-job training presumably increases the future marginal productivity of workers in the firms providing it; general training, however, also increases their marginal product in many other firms as well. Since in a competitive labor market the wage rates paid by any firm are determined by marginal productivities in other firms, future wage rates as well as marginal products would increase in firms providing general training. These firms could capture some of the return from training only if their marginal product rose by more than their wages. "Perfectly general" training would be equally useful in many firms and marginal products would rise by the same extent in all of them. Consequently, wage rates would rise by exactly the same amount as the marginal product and the firms providing such training could not capture any of the return.

Training has an important effect on the relation between earnings and age. Suppose that untrained persons received the same earnings regardless of age, as shown by the horizontal line UU in Picture-1. Trained persons would receive lower earnings during the training period because training is paid for at that time and higher earnings at later ages because the return is collected then. The combined effect of paying for and collecting the return from training in this way would be to make the age-earnings curve of trained persons, shown by TT in Picture-1, steeper than that of untrained persons, the difference being greater the greater the cost of, and return from, the investment. Not only does training make the curve steeper but, as indicated by Picture-1, also more concave; that is, the rate of increase in earnings is affected more at younger than at older ages.

Picture-5.2   Relation of Earnings to Age

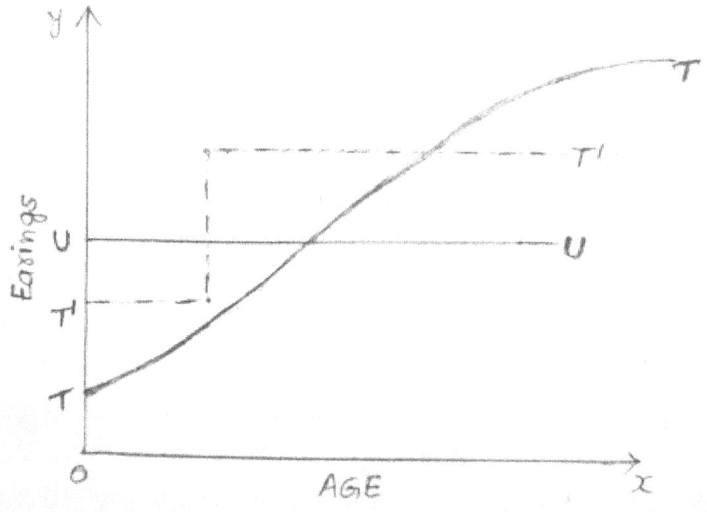

Suppose, to take an extreme case, that training raised the level of marginal productivity but had no effect on the slope, so that the marginal productivity of trained persons was also independent of age. If earnings equaled marginal product, TT would merely be parallel to and higher than UU, showing neither slope nor concavity. Since, however, earnings of trained persons would be below marginal productivity during the training period and equal afterward, they would rise sharply at the end of the training period and then level off (as shown by the dashed line T'T' in Picture-1), imparting a concave appearance to the curve as a whole. In this extreme case an extreme concavity appears (as in TT); in less extreme cases the principle would be the same and the concavity more continuous.

(II)   Specific Training

Completely general training increases the marginal productivity of trainees by exactly the same amount in the firms providing the training as in other firms. Clearly some kinds of training increase productivity by different amounts in the firms providing the training and in other firms. Training that increases productivity more in firms providing it will be called specific training. Completely specific training can be defined as training that has no effect on the productivity of trainees that would be useful in other firms. Much on-the-job training is neither completely specific nor completely general but increases productivity more in the firms providing it and falls within the definition of specific training. The rest increases productivity by at least as much in other firms and falls within a definition of general training. A few illustrations of the scope of specific training are presented before a formal analysis is developed.

The military offers some forms of training that are extremely useful in the civilian sector, as already noted, and others that are only of minor use to civilians, i.e., astronauts, fighter pilots, and missile men. Such training falls within the scope of specific training because productivity is raised in the military but not (much) elsewhere.

Resources are usually spent by firms in familiarizing new employees with their organization, and the knowledge thus acquired is a form of specific training because productivity is raised more in the firms acquiring the knowledge than in other firms. Other kinds of hiring costs, such as employment agency fees, the expenses incurred by new employees in finding jobs, or the time employed in interviewing, testing, checking references, and in bookkeeping do not so obviously increase the knowledge of new employees, but they too are a form of specific investment in human capital, although not training. They are an investment because outlays over a short period create distributed effects on productivity; they are specific because productivity is raised primarily in the firms making the outlays; they are in human capital because they lose their value whenever employees leave

2   *SCHOOLING*

A school can be defined as an institution specializing in the production of training, as distinct from a firm that offers training in conjunction with the production of goods. Some schools, like those for barbers, specialize in one skill, while others, like universities, offer a large and diverse set. Schools and firms are often substitute sources of particular skills. This substitution is evidenced by the shift over time, for instance, in law from apprenticeships in law firms to law schools and in engineering from on-the-job experience to engineering schools. Some types of knowledge can be mastered better if simultaneously related to a practical problem; others require prolonged specialization.

That is, there are complementary elements between learning and work and between learning and time. Most training in the construction industry is apparently still best given on the job, while the training of physicists requires a long period of specialized effort. The development of certain skills requires both specialization and experience and can be had partly from firms and partly from schools.

Physicians receive apprenticeship training as interns and residents after several years of concentrated instruction in medical schools. Or, to take an example closer to home, a research economist spends not only many years in school but also a rather extensive apprenticeship in mastering the "art" of empirical and theoretical research. The complementary elements between firms and schools depend in part on the amount of formalized knowledge available: price theory can be formally presented in a course, while a formal statement of the principles used in gathering and handling empirical materials is lacking. Training in a new industrial skill is usually first given on the job, since firms tend to be the first to be aware of its value, but as demand develops, some of the training shifts to schools. A student does not work for pay while in school but may do so after or before school, or during vacations. His earnings are usually less than if he were not in school since he cannot work as much or as regularly. The difference between what could have been and what is earned (including any value placed on foregone leisure) is an important indirect cost of schooling. Tuition, fees, books, supplies, and unusual transportation and lodging expenses are other, more direct, costs. Net earnings can be defined as the difference between actual earnings and direct school costs.

3   *INFORMATION*

On-the-job and school training are not the only activities that raise real income primarily by increasing the knowledge at a person's command. Information about the prices charged by different sellers would enable a person to buy from the cheapest, thereby raising his command over resources; information about the wages offered by different firms would enable him to work for the firm paying the highest. In both examples, information about the economic system and about consumption and production possibilities is increased, as distinct from knowledge of a particular skill. Information about the political or social system—the effect of different parties or social arrangements—could also significantly raise real incomes.

Let us consider in more detail investment in information about employment opportunities. A better job might be found by spending money on employment agencies and situation-wanted ads, by using one's time to examine want ads, by talking to friends and visiting firms, or in Stigler's language by "search." When the new job requires geographical movement, additional time and resources would be spent in moving. These expenditures constitute an investment in information about job opportunities that would yield a return in the form of higher earnings than would otherwise have been received. If workers paid the costs and collected the return, an investment in search would have the same implications about age-earnings profiles, depreciation, etc., as general on-the-job training and schooling, although it must be noted that the direct costs of search, like the direct costs of schooling, are usually added to consumption rather than deducted from earnings. If firms paid the costs and collected the return, search would have the same implications as on-the-job specific training.

4   *HEALTH*

One way to invest in human capital is to improve emotional and physical health. In Western countries today earnings are much more closely geared to knowledge than to strength, but in an earlier day, and elsewhere still today, strength had a significant influence on earnings. Moreover, emotional health increasingly is considered an important determinant of earnings in all parts of the world. Health, like knowledge, can be improved in many ways. A decline in the death rate at working ages may improve earnings prospects by extending the period during which earnings are received; a better diet adds strength and stamina, and thus earning capacity; or an improvement in working conditions—higher wages, coffee breaks, and so on—may affect morale and productivity.

Firms can invest in the health of employees through medical examinations, lunches, or avoidance of activities with high accident and death rates. An investment in health that increased productivity to the same extent in many firms would be a general investment and would have the same effect as general training; while an investment in health that increased productivity more in the firms making it would be a specific investment and would have the same effect as specific training. Of course, most investments in health are made outside firms, in households, hospitals, and medical offices.

The productivity of employees depends not only on their ability and the amount invested in them both on and off the job but also on their motivation, or the intensity of their work. Economists have long recognized that motivation in turn partly depends on earnings because of the effect of an increase in earnings on morale and aspirations.

It can be concluded from the Becker's theory of human capital that investment in human beings in the form of on-the-job training, schooling, information and health make him/her productive capital for the economy.

MINCER'S THEORY OF HUMAN CAPITAL

Jacob Mincer, Polish-born American economist (born July 15, 1922, Poland—died Aug. 20, 2006, New York), was generally regarded as the father of modern labour economics and helped to define the field with his development and analysis of human capital, the manner in which individuals invest in their job skills to earn larger salaries in the future. Using data from the 1950 and 1960 censuses, Mincer determined that a person's annual earnings increased by 5–10% for each year of additional schooling completed. He was also one of the first economists to examine earnings by women and the role their contribution played in family finances.

During his academic career, Mincer authored four books and hundreds of journal articles, papers and essays. Mincer's ground-breaking work: *Schooling, Experience and Earnings*, published in 1974, used data from the 1950 and 1960 Censuses to relate income distribution in America to the varying amounts of education and on-the-job training among workers. "He calculated, for example, that annual earnings rose by 5 to 10 percent in the 1950s and 1960s for every year of additional schooling. There was a similar, although smaller, return on investment in job training—and age played a role."

Mincer's work continues to have a profound impact on the field of labor economics. Papers in the field frequently use Mincerian equations, which model wages as a function of human capital in statistical estimation. And as a result of Mincer's pioneering work, variables such as schooling and work experience are now the most commonly used measures of human capital.

The Mincer's Earnings Function

The **Mincer earnings function** is a single-equation model that explains wage income as a function of schooling and experience, named after Jacob Mincer. The equation has been examined on many datasets and Thomas Lemieux argues it is ***"one of the most widely used models in empirical economics"***. Typically the logarithm of earnings is modelled as the sum of years of education and a quadratic function of "years of potential experience". Sherwin Rosen, in his article celebrating Mincer's contribution, memorably noted that when data was interrogated using this equation one might describe them as having been ***Mincered***.

The Mincer's (1974) earnings function is the prime analytical tool when it comes to empirically implement the human capital theory. It is the framework used to estimate returns to schooling, returns to schooling quality and to measure the impact of differences in work experience on e.g male-female wage gaps. This equation has become the cornerstone of empirical researches on earnings determinations. In the most widely used version of Mincer's human capital earnings function log earnings are modelled as the sum of a linear function of years of education and a quadratic function of years of potential experience.

Jacob Mincer showed that the human capital model generates age-earnings functions of the form:

$$\mathbf{LnY = \beta 0 + \beta 1S + \beta 2T + \beta 3T^2 + u}$$

Where **S** indicates the number of years of schooling, **T** gives the number of years of labour market experience, $\mathbf{T}^2$ is a quadratic on experience and **Y** is the wage rate. **β0** is related to initial earnings capacity, **β1** is the rate of return to education, **β2** and β3 are related to both the amount and the financial return to on-job-training, **u** is the error term.

Mincer's earnings function yields at least three important empirical implications. The first is that earnings levels are related to human capital investments. This means that the more human capital investments an individual makes the higher his or her earnings. Second, the earnings function is concave^2. It implies that earnings rise more quickly for the young, then earnings growth decreases gradually in the middle ages. The third is related to the social return which highlights any spillover effects and includes transfers and taxes.

The Mincer equation—arguably the most widely used in empirical work—can be used to explain a host of economic, and even non-economic, phenomena. One such application involves explaining (and estimating) employment earnings as a function of schooling and labor market experience. The Mincer equation provides estimates of the average monetary returns of one additional year of education. This information is important for policymakers who must decide on education spending, prioritization of schooling levels, and education financing programs such as student loans.

The Mincer equation suggests that each additional year of education produces a private (i.e. individual) rate of return to schooling of about 5–8% per year, ranging from a low of 1% to more than 20% in some countries. Globally, the returns to tertiary education are highest, followed by primary and then secondary schooling; this represents a significant reversal from many studies' prior results. Policymakers can learn much from Mincerian results; for instance, further expansion of university education appears to be very worthwhile for the individual, meaning that governments need to find ways to make financing more readily available, and that high rates of return are found through investment in girls' education.

Picture 5.3. Global average of returns to schooling

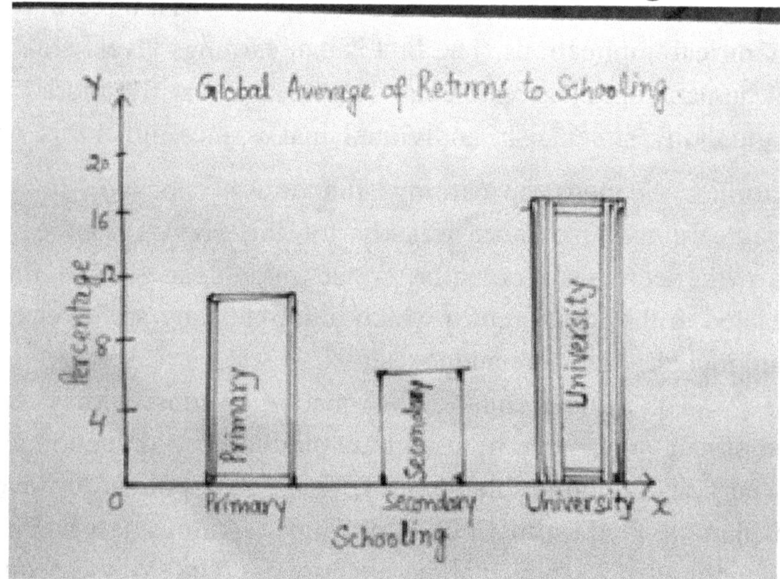

Source: Montenegro, C. E., and H. A. Patrinos, *Comparable Estimates of Returns to Schooling around the World*, World Bank Policy Research Working Paper No. 7020, 2014 [7].

Importance of the Model

The Mincer equation explains earnings as a function of schooling and labor market experience, giving a clear sense of the average monetary returns of one additional year of schooling.

The rate of return to investment in schooling is presented in a simple and comparable format that permits estimates of the profitability of schooling, thus allowing people to use this information for investment decision purposes.

The interest in ascertaining the value of the investment in education has increased over time. Worldwide, education spending has increased from 3.6% of GDP in 1970 to more than 4.8% of GDP in 2011. At the same time, individuals and their families invest a significant amount out of their own pockets for tuition and other education-related expenses. The student's foregone earnings represent the largest costs incurred by individuals and their families while studying. Is this massive investment in schooling justified? One way to analyze this question is to estimate the costs and benefits of the investment, for which the Mincer equation is ideally suited.

Although most rate of return studies attempt to estimate the returns to schooling for a country, region, or level of schooling, lately there has been interest in more disaggregated information such as returns for certain population groups categorized according to specific characteristic, e.g. ethnic, linguistic, religious groups, persons with disabilities, and so on. Estimating Mincer equations for different groups such as males and females or ethnic groups can be used to study the extent of labor market discrimination. Returns to schooling for women are used to justify further investments in girls' schooling. Returns to schooling in developing countries are used to justify international goals for getting all children into school. In developed countries, the massive investments in higher education, rising tuition levels, and increasing student debt loads are calling into question the overall attractiveness of educational investment.

Criticism

1 The relationship between schooling and earnings does not necessarily imply causality.

2 Earnings functions provide private (i.e. individual) returns to schooling, whereas government/public costs and other benefits are needed to estimate social rates of return.

3 As economies become more complex and technological developments alter the demand for education, decades-old cross-sectional data may not be informative about returns to current investment decisions.

Conclusion

The Mincer equation has clearly helped advance the fields of labor and educational economics. It has improved the understanding of the determinants of earnings, the rate of return to schooling, the demand for education, the impacts of discrimination, and the importance of labor market experience and on-the-job training. Moreover, the simple Mincer equation is now being used in other fields such as sociology and anthropology. The Mincer equation is thus a genuinely valuable tool for a wide-ranging group of researchers and policymakers; it should be relied upon extensively for determining educational return estimates and will continue to contribute many other policy relevant fields in the future.

CHISWICK'S MODEL

Barry R. Chiswick is Professor and Chair of the Department of Economics at the Columbian College of Arts and Sciences (CCAS), George Washington University (since 2011). Professor Chiswick has an international reputation for his research in Labor Economics, Human Resources, the Economics of Immigration, the Economics of Minorities, the Economics of Language, Economics of Religion, and Income Distribution. He is recognized as having done the seminal research on the Economics of Immigration, and continues to be the leader in the field.

His most-cited research article, published in 1978, analyzes the earnings of foreign-born adult white men by comparing these earnings with those of native born men as well as among foreign born men by country of origin, years in the United States, and citizenship and explores differences in the effects of schooling and post-school training, using 1970 U.S. census data. His research finds that immigrants' earnings to rise more rapidly with U.S. labor market experience than those of native born, although immigrants initially earn less than their native counterparts, resulting in immigrants' earnings exceeding those of native born after 10 to 15 years, independent of the immigrants' citizenship.

He stated that after immigrants arrive in the US they gradually acquire knowledge of the language, customs, and the nature of labour markets in the US. He found earnings increased, although at a decreasing rate, with the number of years an immigrant.

Chiswick (1978) analyzed the earnings of immigrant adult white men in the US. He took a cross section of data, from the 1970 census of population, giving a snap shot of the US population at this time. This allowed Chiswick to compare the current earnings of newly arrived immigrants with the current earnings of immigrants who arrived years before. He analysed these earnings through comparisons with the native born and among the foreign born by country of origin, years in the United States and citizenship. Differences in the effects of schooling and post school training were also explored.

Picture 5.4

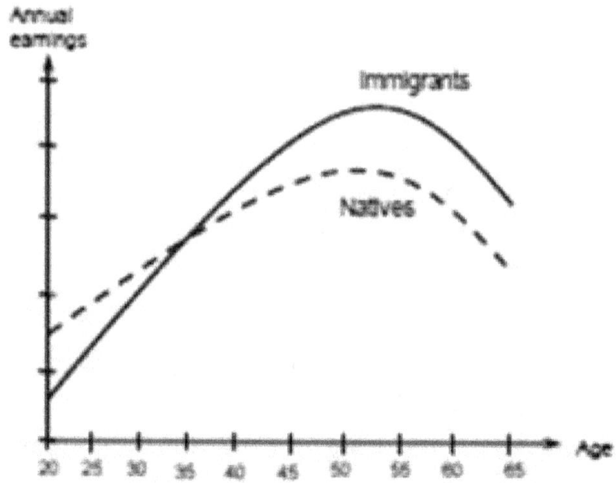

Chiswick's (1978) cross section data set gave three distinct results when looking at the Age-earnings profiles of immigrant and native men.

1. Immigrant earnings are initially lower than native men.
2. The immigrant age-earnings profile is steeper than the native age-earnings profile, the earnings of the foreign born are growing at a faster rate.
3. After 10 -15 years in the US immigrants earn more than natives.

Chiswick's study (1978), offers the following explanations for the results:

1. As there are aspects of schooling that are country specific, a year of schooling prior to immigration will have a smaller effect on earnings than a year of schooling for the native born.
2. As there are aspects of labour market that are country specific, a year of experience prior to immigration has a smaller effect on earnings than a year of experience prior

to immigration has a smaller effect on earnings than a year of experience for a native person. Therefore upon arriving in the country and gaining more experience in US immirants earnings will rise quickly.

3. As immigrants initially have less human capital specific to the United States than natives - born persons of the same schooling and age, just after they arrive their earnings are lower than the native born.

4. After they arrive, as immigrants make investments in post school training informally acquire "experience" living in the United States, the earnings of immigrants rise at a faster rate than the earnings of the native born.

5. As immigrants have the incentive to make their largest adjustment investments just after they arrive, the absolute decline in the "knowledge gap" between immigrants and the native born is sharpest in these years. The rise in earnings with time in the United States is steepest in the first few years.

6. Immigrants make investments in post - school training relevant for jobs in the US. These investments initially depress earnings and raise them later on. This can be seen on the age earnings profile.

7. Becker (1964) has shown that for the same total investment in training, experience earnings profiles are steeper the smaller the proportion that is firm specific and the smaller the proportion of firm- specific training that is financed by the employer. Chiswick(1978) stated that theforeign born were more likely to have training which was not firm specific or financed by the employer because employers have poorer knowledge of them than the native born. The experience immigrants therefore gain has a larger effect on their earnings.

8. The effect on earnings of time in the United States, holding total labour market experience constant, is weaker for immigrants from countries that more closely resemble the United States.

9. The foreign born may have more innate ability, are more highly motivated toward labour market success, or self - finance larger investments in post school training. These high earning, Chiswick believed, are a consequence of self - selection explain why eventually immigrants earnings overtake those of natives.

Chiswick explains the smaller effect of pre-immigration schooling by the fact that knowledge acquired at school may be country specific and provide employers in the US with poor information. It could also be explained by the lower possibility of lower quality of foreign schooling.

Chiswick also found a smaller effect of post-immigration schooling for foreign born men. He discussed that this may be due in part to self- selection in migration, stating that maybe only the most able and most highly motivated of those with little schooling migrate while those with higher levels of schooling (or who subsequently acquire) came from a broader ability and motivation spectrum.

ECONOMICS OF HEALTH AND NUTRITION

Health economics is a branch of economics concerned with issues related to efficiency, effectiveness, value and behavior in the production and consumption of health and healthcare. In broad terms, health economists study the functioning of healthcare systems and health-affecting behaviors such as smoking.

A seminal 1963 article by **Kenneth Arrow**, often credited with giving rise to health economics as a discipline, drew conceptual distinctions between health and other goods. Factors that distinguish health economics from other areas include extensive government intervention, intractable uncertainty in several dimensions, asymmetric information, barriers to entry, externalities and the presence of a third-party agent. In healthcare, the third-party agent is the physician, who makes purchasing decisions (e.g., whether to order a lab test, prescribe a medication, perform a surgery, etc.) while being insulated from the price of the product or service.

Health economics is the study of how scarce resources are allocated among alternative uses for the care of sickness and the promotion, maintenance and improvement of health, including the study of how health care and health-related services, their costs and benefits, and health itself are distributed among individuals and groups in society. It can, broadly, be defined as 'the application of the theories, concepts and techniques of economics to the health sector' (Lee and Mills, 1983)

Health economists evaluate multiple types of financial information: costs, charges and expenditures.

Uncertainty is intrinsic to health, both in patient outcomes and financial concerns. The knowledge gap that exists between a physician and a patient creates a situation of distinct advantage for the physician, which is called *asymmetric information.*

Externalities arise frequently when considering health and health care, notably in the context of infectious disease. For example, making an effort to avoid catching the common cold affects people other than the decision maker.

The demand for healthcare is a derived demand from the demand for health. Healthcare is demanded as a means for consumers to achieve a larger stock of "health capital." The demand for health is unlike most other goods because individuals allocate resources in order to both consume and produce health.

The above description gives three roles of persons in health economics. The World Health Report states that people take four roles in the healthcare:

1. Contributors
2. Citizens
3. Provider
4. Consumers

MARKET OF HEALTHCARE

The standard theory of how markets work is the model of supply and demand, in which buyers and sellers are guided by prices to an efficient allocation of resources. That market has several notable features:

1. The main interested parties are the buyers and sellers in the market.
2. Buyers are good judges of what they get from sellers.
3. Buyers pay sellers directly for the goods and services being exchanged.
4. Market prices are the primary mechanism for coordinating the decisions of market participants.
5. The invisible hand, left to its own devices, leads to an efficient allocation of resources.

For many goods and services in the economy, this model offers a reasonably good description, yet none of these five features of the standard model reflects what goes on in the market for healthcare. Like other markets, the healthcare market has consumers (patients) and producers (doctors, nurses, etc.). But various features of this market complicate the analysis of their interactions. In particular:

1. Third parties—insurers, governments, and unwitting bystanders—often have an interest in healthcare outcomes.

2. Patients often don't know what they need and cannot evaluate the treatment they are getting.

3. Healthcare providers are often paid not by the patients but by private or government health insurance.

4. The rules established by these insurers, more than market prices, determine the allocation of resources.

5. In light of the foregoing four points, the invisible hand can't work its magic, and so the allocation of resources in the healthcare market can end up highly inefficient

Healthcare is not the only good or service in the economy that departs from the standard model of supply, demand, and the invisible hand. (Recall our discussions of externalities and monopoly.) But healthcare may be the most important good or service that departs so radically from this benchmark. Examining the special features of this market is a good starting point for understanding why the government plays a large role in the provision of healthcare and why health policy is often complex and vexing.

There are both positive and normative ways of looking at the problem in health economics.

The normative issues relate to what should be, for example, what should be the appropriate budget allocation for HIV/AIDS control. The positive branch of health economics applies all modern micro economic theory in health care/medical care. Demand for health care that depends on the income of the individual, his/her taste, public and private supply of health care, etc is a subject matter in positive health economics.

Scope of Health Economics

The scope of health economics is neatly encapsulated by Alan Williams' "plumbing diagram" (picture-1) dividing the discipline into eight distinct topics:

- What influences health? (other than healthcare)
- What is health and what is its value?
- The demand for healthcare
- The supply of healthcare
- Micro-economic evaluation at treatment level
- Market equilibrium
- Evaluation at whole system level
- Planning, budgeting and monitoring mechanisms.

Picture-5.5 *Scope of Health Economics*

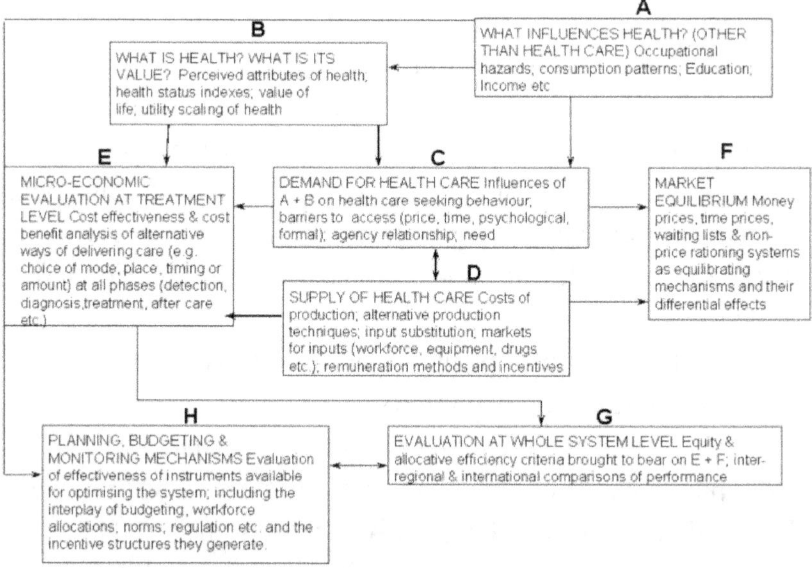

Significance of health economics

Health economics is becoming a subject of increasing significance particularly in the developing countries primarily because of:

(i)   an economic climate where resources are extremely scare and decisions on priorities are crucial but difficult;

(ii)   a growing appreciation among health professionals and policy-makers that health economics and economists can help them formulate policies and make decisions;

(iii)   the increasing maturity of the sub-disciplines of health economics; and

(iv)   the growing of interest among economists and others in applying their economic skills to health issues (Lee and Mills, 1983a).

Currently, the task before economists is to elicit the valuations which may be useful to formulate health services policy. **First**, it might be in the form of demand studies, or by trying to discover what policy makers' preferences are. **Second**, there is a need to establish the true costs of delivering health care or to estimate all real costs like the use of patients' time, loss of output elsewhere in the system etc. **Third**, it is necessary to evaluate the relative costs and benefits of particular policy options. **Fourth**, the effects of certain economic variables like user charges, time and distance costs of accessibility, etc on the utilization of health services may be estimated. **Fifth**, planning and budgeting systems and possible changes therein in health care delivery system are to be made. Table 1 presents an overview of relevant health issues and consequent tasks of economists to address them.

■

CHAPTER – 6
BRAIN DRAIN: MEANING, CAUSES AND EFFECTS

Brain drain can be described as the process in which a country loses its most educated and talented workers to other countries through migration. This trend is considered a problem, because the most highly skilled and competent individuals leave the country, and contribute their expertise to the economy of other countries. The country they leave can suffer economic hardships because those who remain don't have the 'know-how' to make a difference.

Brain drain can also be defined as the loss of the academic and technological labour force through the moving of human capital to more favourable geographic, economic, or professional environments. More often than not, the movement occurs from developing countries to developed countries or areas.

Definitions of Brain Drain

1.   As per **Cambridge Dictionary-** *"the situation in which large numbers of educated and very skilled people leave their own country to live and work in another one where pay and conditions are better".*

2.   According to **Frederic Docquier** the term *"brain drain" refers to the international transfer of human capital resources, and it applies mainly to the migration of highly educated individuals from developing to developed countries.*

3.   According to **Oxford Advanced Learner's dictionary,** *"Brain Drain is the movement of highly skilled and*

qualified people to a country where they can work in better conditions and earn more money".

CAUSES OF BRAIN DRAIN

There are various causes of brain drain, but they differ depending on the country that's experiencing it. The main causes include seeking employment or higher paying jobs, political instability, and to seek a better quality of life. Causes of brain drain can categorized into push factors and pull factors.

The **push factors** are negative characteristics of the home country that forms the impetus for intelligent people migrating from *Lesser Developed Countries* (LDC). In addition to unemployment and political instability, some other push factors are the absence of research facilities, employment discrimination, economic underdevelopment, lack of freedom, and poor working conditions.

Pull factors are the positive characteristics of the developed country from which the migrant would like to benefit. Higher paying jobs and a better quality of life are examples of pull factors. Other pull factors include superior economic outlook, the prestige of foreign training, relatively stable political environment, a modernized educational system to allow for superior training, intellectual freedom, and rich cultures. These lists are not complete; there may be other factors, some of which can be specific to countries or even to individuals.

The following factors lead to brain drain from developing countries like India to developed countries like the USA:

1   In developing countries, job opportunities are limited or no-existent. So highly qualified persons migrate to developed countries like U.S.A. to take advantage of wider and better job opportunities.

2   Even though similar skills are needed in both developing and developed countries, people migrate and settle permanently in the latter countries because they pay very high salaries. The famous saying is "brains go to where money is."

3   Some persons go abroad for higher studies and research because academic and research facilities are not of international standards in poor countries. For instants, there are first rate facilities for research in social and natural sciences and technology. These attract persons from poor countries who after acquiring higher proficiency in their respective fields permanently settle there. Another saying is "Brains go where brains are."

4   A few highly skilled person migrate and settle permanently in developed countries attracted by a comfortable standard of living as compared to their own country.

5   Some are persuaded by friends and relatives already settled abroad to get higher education and training. They ultimately settle in that country by joining firms in their respective fields of study.

6   Another important factor is the excess supply specialised and trained persons at home over the demand for them in developed countries which encourages people to migrate to developed countries permanently.

7   Brain drain is also encouraged in developing countries because of "unfriendly, non-motivated, constrained and non-creative work environment" as compared to friendly, cooperative and healthy work environment in developed countries.

8   In developing countries good jobs are filled and promotions are made on the basis of family connections, political influence and corruption. In public sector

institutions and organisations, there is **"Stifling and unresponsive bureaucracy."** Corruption is rampant which encourages brain drain abroad. On the other hand, freedom of occupation, better job opportunities, possibilities of professional growth, financial security and congenial work environment attract highly qualified and skilled personnel to developed countries.

9   Countries like the United States lure away talented manpower from developing countries by liberalising their immigration policies to permit and encourage such migration.

EFFECTS OF BRAIN DRAIN ON THE HOME COUNTRY

When brain drain is prevalent in a developing country, there may be some negative repercussions that can affect the economy. These effects include but are not limited to:

- Loss of tax revenue
- Loss of potential future entrepreneurs
- A shortage of important, skilled workers
- The exodus may lead to loss of confidence in the economy, which will cause persons to desire to leave rather than stay
- Loss of innovative ideas
- Loss of the country's investment in education
- The loss of critical health and education services

Brain drain is usually described as a problem that needs to be solved. However, there are benefits that can be derived from the phenomena. When people move from LDC countries to developed countries, they learn new skills and expertise, which they can utilize to the advantage of the home economy once they return. Another benefit is remittances; the migrants send the money they earn back to the home country, which can help to stimulate the home country's economy.

MEASURES TO REDUCE BRAIN DRAIN:

The following measures have been suggested by economists to reduce brain drain from developing countries:

1. Prof. **Parthasarathi** in an article "Brain in Developing Countries" suggests that every student should be allowed to go for higher study abroad only if he has attained the highest possible level of education in his chosen field of study in his own country. After this, he should be employed in the country for at least two years before being permitted to go abroad.

2. **Prof. Dandekar** in an article "The Brain Drain" suggests that the inequality within the intellectual ranks both in terms of status and income, should be narrowed down to reduce brain drain.

3. Besides, "an intellectually stimulating environment" should be created in the institutions where the talented persons work in the home country.

4. An organisation should be set up to provide information and advice to highly qualified persons on job opportunities within the country.

5. There should be a Scientists Pool Scheme to help the young talented scientists for placements in various institutions and organisations and to attract those who are working or studying abroad to come back to their country.

6. Besides good pay and perks, they should be provided such amenities as housing, schooling for children, conveyance, etc. For those who are willing to return from abroad should also be paid the travel fare by the organisation which they join.

7   **Prof. Jagdish Bhagwati** suggests the levy of an international tax on professionals settling abroad. The country to which the person migrates permanently should collect this tax and remit it to the country from which the person comes. Such a tax would be sufficient to close the revenue deficits of developing countries.

Recently, Mihir Desai, Devesh Kapur and John McHale of Harvard University have empirically carried forward Bhagwati's idea of the immigration tax. They have estimated that the net fiscal loss of India from emigration of skilled persons to the USA was between 0.24 per cent and 0.58 per cent of India's GDP in 2001.

According to them, a Bhagwati Tax can yield an annual revenue of about $ 500 million. They prefer an "exit tax" on all skilled persons who emigrate. But the problem is of collecting such a tax – when, where and how?

8   Prof. Bhagwati has also suggested the setting up a world migration organisation on the lines of WTO to develop a coherent policy on the movement of individuals across borders.

Above all, to prevent brain drain and to attract those who have already settled abroad, it is essential that there is a congenial working environment which provides financial security, professional growth, based on meritocracy and is free from bureaucratic corruption and nepotism.

Coming back home of successful emigrants, some of whom get fabulously rich, will invest capital to start industries in developing countries, thereby leading to reverse brain drain.

■

CHAPTER – 7
MIGRATION: MEANING, CAUSES AND EFFECTS

INTRODUCTION

Migration means movement or shift of people from one place to another. People move from one place to another for temporary or permanent settlement due to social, political & religious reasons.

Globalisation has made migration of people easy & common.

TYPES OF MIGRATION:

The following are the different types of migration:-

1. Local Migration:-

It involves movement of people from one locality to another.

2. Regional Migration:-

It involves movement of people from one region to another.

3. Rural to Urban Migration:-

It involves movement of people from rural areas to cities areas due to industrialization.

4. Urban to Rural Migration:-

It involves movement of people from urban areas to rural areas due to higher cost of urban living.

5. Mars Migration:-

It refers to the movement of large group of people from one geographical area to another.

6. Forced Migration:-

It refers to forced movement of people away from their

home against their will due to violence, natural calamities or communal rights.

CAUSES OF MIGRATION:-

1. Economic factors:-

Unemployment and poverty forced people to migrate from one place to another. Rural people migrate to cities in search of employment opportunities for better salaries, incentives, higher standard of living.

2. Social factors:-

Migration may also take place due to social factors such as family, marriage, children, etc. After marriage a girl has to migrate from her place of resident to her husband place & if a child decide to study elsewhere, the parents also migrate to the place where the child decide to study.

3. Environmental factors:-

Natural disasters such as flood, famine, earth quack, etc compel people to migrate to safer places.

4. Medical factors:-

Some people experience poor health conditions due to unsuitable climate and high population level, due to this, they migrate from one place to another for better medical & health care facilities.

5. Political factors:-

Political migration takes place due to political instability, communalism, linguism, regionalism, riots, terrorism, etc. which creates conflicts & violence in cities & states. Thus, political factors lead to migration of people to the place where there is proper law & order.

EFFECTS OF MIGRATION:-

1. Brain Drain:-

There has been migration of Indian professionals, academicians, scientists, engineers,etc to foreign countries. Due to which their talent, knowledge & skills are denied to our country's growth & development.

Therefore, our country should undertake effective planning to solve the problem of brain drain.

2. Increase of foreign exchange reserves:-

When people migrate to foreign countries, earned foreign currency & sent it to their family in home country. There is an increase in foreign exchange reserve of the home country.

3. Fusion of cultures:-

International migration leads to fusion of culture due to exchange of cultural traits such as food habits, dressing style, language, etc which results in change of lifestyle & personality of the migrant.

4. Hostilities towards migrants:-

The migrants have to face hostilities from local people, who may not treat them well and they may even harm their life & property leading to torture & harassment.

5. Social & psychological problems:-

Migration leads to social problems such as overcrowding of people, growth of slumps, increases crimes & evils, spread of diseases, etc.

When people migrate to different places leaving behind their family, relatives & friends, they feel lonely, isolated and insecure which leads to many psychological problems.

THEORIES AND APPROACHES TO MIGRATION

Various attempts towards defining the process of migration and the consequent conceptualisation of the phenomena have resulted in the emergence of a number of theories and philosophical approaches. But the review of theories and approaches reveal that so far there has not evolved a framework or theoretical expression that gained universal acceptance.

Though, a comprehensive and widely accepted theory is not evolved, scholars of migration have tried to formulate theories based on various aspects of migration. As regards the genesis of migration, some works concentrate on the decision making of individuals and others focus on society – *micro analytical* and *macro-analytical* respectively. Some other works used the terms *humanist* and *determinist* to denote the same. In *humanist* approach, the individual is the decision maker in the choice whether to migrate or not. In contrast, for the *determinist*, it is the society where he lives becomes the crucial factor. Still, some other studies have tried to integrate the determinist and humanist approaches. Theories of migration are important in the sense that they help those who study human mobility within wider political, social, economic and cultural contexts.

1 Determinist Approaches of Human Migration
Empirical Laws

Ravenstein, a German born former cartographer for the British war office is remembered as the pioneer who formulated a theoretical foundation for the migration study. His hypothesis were first published in the Geographical Magazine of 1876 in which he reacted against the view of an earlier demographer, W. Farr, who remarked that migration occurs without any definite law. Later, Ravenstein published two papers in the Journal of the Statistical Society in June 1886 and June 1889. The first paper was the result of an extensive study of British Census's Place of Birth Tables of 1871 and 1881 and the second paper on the basis of data from 20 other countries of North America and Europe. A summary of laws as appeared in these papers is given below.

1. Most of the migrants go only a short distance.
2. Migrants moving long distance generally go by preference to one of the great centres of commerce and industry.
3. Migration proceeds in a series of steps.
4. Urban people are less migratory than rural people.
5. Females are more migratory than males in short distances, but males predominate over long distances.
6. Each migration current produces a compensating counter current, but the former pre-dominates the latter.
7. Families hardly move over long distance.
8. The development of commerce and industry and the improvement of transport facilities lead to increase in volume of migration.
9. Direction of migration is largely from agricultural regions to industrial areas.
10. The important reason behind the decision to migrate is economic.

Though Ravenstein's laws have attracted critical appraisals from various corners8 he remains the pioneer and one of the pre-eminent migration theorist, who started the theory of migration ball rolling, who provided the base upon which subsequent migration research and theorizing were put up. Notwithstanding, some 20th century scholars have tried to give the laws of

Ravenstein some theoretical credence by explaining and verifying the laws on the basis of Newton's Law of Gravity.9 His law that females are more migratory than males in short migration is not true in many migration streams of various ages and regions. Migration occuring in series is also not having enough base. However, as Everett S.Lee rightly remarks- *"In the three quarters of a century which have passed, Ravenstein has been much quoted and occasionally challenged"*. But while there have been literally thousands of migration studies in the meantime *few additional generalisations have been advanced.* True, there have been studies of age and migration, sex and migration, race and migration, distance and migration, education and migration, the labour force and migration and so forth. But most studies which focused upon the characteristics of migrants have been conducted with little reference to the volume of migration and few studies have considered the reasons for migration on the assimilation of migrants at the destination.

2   Capital Maximisation Approaches
Neo-Classical Theories

A number of early theories on migration process surrounds around *neoclassical economics.* According to this, migration occurs as a result of the rational economic calculation of the workers of the wage differentials, which results in the spatial mobility of workers from low-wage to high-wage areas.

Migration was thus labour reallocation in response to market need. It was the experience of high volume of rural – urban migration in 1960s in many developing nations despite rising levels of urban unemployment that tempted Michael Todaro to formulate his theory in 1969.

According to **Todaro,** migration proceeds in response to urban-rural differences in 'expected rather than actual earnings'. Migrants as decision makers consider the various labour market opportunities available to them as between, say, the rural and urban sectors, and chose the one, which maximizes their 'expected' gains from migration. Expected gains are measured by a) the difference in real incomes between rural and urban job opportunities and b) the probability of a new migrant obtaining an urban job. In short, there are four essential features for Todaro model.

1)   Migration is stimulated primarily by rational economic consideration of relative benefits and costs, mostly financial but also psychological.

2)   The decision to migrate depends on 'expected' rather than actual rural real wage differentials where the 'expected' differential is determined by the interaction of two variables, the actual urban-rural wage differential and the probability of successfully obtaining employment in the urban modern sector.

3)   The probability of obtaining an urban job is inversely related to the urban unemployment rate.

4)   Migration in excess of urban job opportunity growth rates are not only possible but also rational and probable in the face of continued positive urban-rural 'expected' income differentials.

The advantage of Todaro model is that it admits the urban unemployment. He also thinks all the rural- urban migration occurs not merely on the basis of expectation or probability. The ignorance of urban situation on the part of the migrant may also leads to migration. One important drawback of Todaro model is that it ignores the non-economic factors.

Arthur Lewis (1954) gave a development touch to the migration theory while considering the process of rural – urban labour transfer. Later the study was formalised and extended by John Fei and Gustav Ranis (Fei and Ranis 1061). The Lewis – Fei - Ranis (L – F – R) became the received 'general' theory of the development process in ' labour surplus' Third world nations during most of the late 1950s and 1960s. In the LFR Model, the economy consists of two sectors a) a traditional, 'rural, subsistence sector' characterized by zero or very low productivity 'surplus' labour and b) a high productivity modern 'urban industrial sector' into which labour from the subsistence sector is gradually transferred.

Michael P Todaro has pointed out three handicaps to LFR Model.

1   the Model implicitly assumes that the rate of labour transfer and employment creation is proportional to the rate of capital accumulation.

2   the assumption that surplus labour exists in rural areas and there is full employment in urban areas is also not true.

3   the third key assumption at variance with reality is the notion of the continued existence of constant real urban wages until the supply of rural surplus labour is exhausted.

The theory is interested only in rural – urban migration occurring in a dual economy and it wholly ignores other streams of migration. Further, the subsequent experience of developing countries belied this theory as the industrial sector did not generate sufficient jobs to absorb the migrants from the countryside.

3   Behavioural Decision-making Approaches

Unlike the previous approaches, which focused on spatial analysis, the behavioural approaches investigate how psychological process of cognition and decision making mediate between the environment and the individual. According to Wolpert, migration takes place when the 'place utility' in a few location becomes greater than that of the present location. The concept of place utility is defined as "the net composite of utilities which are derived from the individual's integration at some time and space... May be expressed as a positive or negative quality expressing respectively the individual's satisfaction or dissatisfaction with respect to that place". Wolpert thus became a key figure in the evolution of behavioural approaches. Peoples migrate to a place that provide a high overall place utility than either the origin or alternative destination. The behavioural approach also introduced the concept of 'stress'. Accordingly, in the present location satisfying human will may put up with hardship or stress to a certain extent. But when the stress crosses this limit he decides to migrate.

Everett S. Lee presented his paper at the Annual meeting of Mississippi Valley Historical Association, Kansas City on 23 April, 1965. In the three quarters of a century since Ravenstein presented his hypotheses, little was the development in the field of migration theory. The sum total of the contributions were a) the generalisations made by Dorothy Swaine Thomas and her associates that migrants tended to be adults and persons in their late teens. b) Bogue and Hagood summed up the current state of knowledge under the heading 'An Approach to a Theory of differential migration' and Ottis Durant Duncon wrote a paper on 'the theory and consequences of farm population. Most other essays in migration theory have dealt with advance Mathematical formulations of the relationships between migration and distance.

4   Historical Structural Approach

Prominent exponents of this approach are Portes, Balan, Cardoz, Mangalam *et al*. According to them, any study on migration must "probe into the pressures and counter- -pressures both internal and external to the economy which cause changes in the organisation of production." The Social Organisational Theory put forward by Mangalam (1968) also corroborates to this approach. He sees migration as an agent of social change. According to him, migration is a system with which three elements, society of origin, society of destination, and migrants are inter – dependent and inter (working). In this inter working, each community undergoes social change which is described as the "difference between social organisation of a given society at two different points of time, comprising changes in any or all the three component systems namely the culture, social and personality systems." So migration is not independent endeavours made by individuals; rather it is a part of socio – economic changes that a society experiences. Migration "is an adaptive process whose major objective is maintaining the dynamic equilibrium of a social organisation with a minimum of change and at the same time providing those members ways to overcome the deprivation."

Though historical approach connect migration to socio – political and economic changes that a society experiences through years it pays no consideration to individual factors in the process of decision – making. Related to historical structural approach, there is the Marxian structural approach. They assign the forces behind the migration on the *hidden logic* of the capitalist mode of production. Any explanation of migration cannot rely solely on either measuring characteristics of origin and destination locations, as suggested by the capital maximization model, or concentrating on the actions and priorities of individuals, as suggested by the behavioural model. Primary attention must be paid to how the capitalist economy operates and evolves overtime.

5   System Approach

Some have conceived migration as a system in which migration is viewed as circular inter – dependent and self – modifying system in which the effects of changes in one part has a ripple effect through the whole system.

Mabogunje, after his study of rural – urban migration in Africa has presented a paper 'A System Approach to a Theory of Rural – urban Mgration' (1970). According to him migration system is made up of three basic element; Firstly, the migrant who is urged to leave the rural sector by incentives from the surroundings. Secondly, there are certain institutions that control and direct the degree of migration flow. Thirdly, various social, economic and political forces play major role in the process. Although Mabogunje's study is concerned with rural – urban migration in Africa, the conceptualisation has a wider application.

Taylor's Migration Zone Theory is based on his study of diffusion of population from the cradle land of Central Asia, which lies near the Caspian and Aral seas. According to this theory, the first settlers were born in this cradle land and with the origin of later races in this area the former migrated to the outside area forming the marginal fringe of central core. In this hierarchy, first of all the Negrito evolved which was forced to migrate towards the periphery by the Negro who evolved later on. Later on Australoid evolved, which forced former two to migrate towards the periphery. In this way several races were evolved and migrated all over the world. In support of his theory, Taylor has made the following propositions.

1) There has been a centrifugal movement of population from Central Asia to its nearest peninsulas e.g. Eurafrica, Australia and the Americas.

2) There are several racial zones in each and every continent, which is primitive as far as we go away from Central Asia, which give clear-cut evidences of successive migrations of people in each every continent.

3) Primitive races are found in the peripheral areas e.g. Negritoes are found in Tansania, Cape Colony, Green Land, and Brazil. This shows the successive migration of Negrito people to the peripheral areas of the world.

Stouffer formulated the theory of intervening opportunities in 1940. By asserting that the "degree of migration would be inversely related to the distance between the two places as also the extent of intervening opportunities, but directly related to the opportunities in the two places". He criticised the Zipf formulation of distance. He further argues "there is no relationship between mobility and distance….. the number of persons going over a given distance is directly proportional to the number of opportunities at that distance and inversely proportional to the number of intervening opportunities. The relation between mobility and distance may be said to depend on an auxiliary relationship, which express the cumulated (intervening) opportunities as a function of distance".

■

CHAPTER – 8
DEMAND AND SUPPLY FORECASTING OF HR

The important phase of human resource planning is forecasting demand and supply of HR. Forecasting demand involves determining the numbers and kinds of personnel that an organization will need at some point in the future. Most managers consider several factors when forecasting future personnel needs. The demand for the organization's product or service is paramount.

Forecasting supply involves determining what personnel will be available. The two sources are internal and external: people already employed by the firm and those outside the organization.

HR DEMAND FORECASTING:

Demand forecasting is a quantitative aspect of human resource planning. It is the process of estimating the future requirement of human resources of all kinds and types of the organisation.

FACTORS:

Forecasting of demand for human resources depends on certain factors such as:

(1) Employment trend in the organisation for at least last five years to be traced to determine the future needs.

(2) Organisation has to find out the replacement needs due to retirement, death, resignation, termination etc.

(3) Improvement in productivity is yet another factor. To improve productivity organisation needs better employees with skills and potential. Productivity leads to growth but depends on the demands for the product of the enterprise

in the market. Higher demand may lead to more employment of skilled personnel's.

(4) Expansion of the organisation leads to hiring of more skilled persons. The base of human resource forecast is the annual budget. Manufacturing plan depends upon the budget. Expansion in production leads to more hiring of skills and technology.

METHODS OF HR DEMAND FORECASTING:

There are three major methods of demand forecasting. They are as follows.

(1) Executive Judgment:

Executive or Managerial Judgment method is the most suitable for smaller enterprises because they do not afford to have work study technique. Under this method the executives sit together and determine the future manpower requirements of the enterprise and submit the proposal to the top management for approval. This approach is known as 'bottom up' approach.

Sometimes the members of top management sit together and determine the needs on the advice of personnel department. The forecasts so prepared sent for review to the departmental heads and after their consent approved the need. This is known as 'top down' approach. The best way is the combination of the two approaches. Executives at both levels equipped with guidelines sit together and determine the human resources need of the organization.

(2) Work Load Forecasting:

It is also known as work load analysis. Under this method the stock of workload and the continuity of operations are determined. Accordingly the labour requirement is determined. The workload becomes the base for workforce analysis for the forthcoming years. Here due consideration is given to absenteeism and labour turnover. This method is also known as work study technique. Here working capacity of each employee is calculated in terms of man-hours. Man-hours required for each unit is calculated and then number of required employees is calculated.

The example is given below:

(a) Planned annual production = 2, 00,000 units

(b) Standard man-hours required for each unit = 2 Hours

(c) Planned man-hour needed for the year (a x b) = 4, 00,000 hrs.

(d) Planned annual contribution of an employee = 2000 hrs.

(e) No. of employees required ————- (c/d) = 4, 00,000/2000 = 200

This method is useful for long term forecasting.

(3) Statistical Techniques:

Long range demand forecasting for human resources is more responsive to statistical and mathematical techniques. With the help of computers any data is rapidly analyzed.

The following are the methods of forecasting used under this category:

(a) Ratio Trends Analysis:

Under this method the ratios are calculated for the past data related to number of employees of each category i.e. production, sales and marketing levels, work load levels. Future production and sales levels, work load, activity levels are estimated with an allowance of changes in organization, methods and jobs. The future ratios are estimated. Then future human resources requirement is calculated on the basis of established ratios. This method is easy to understand. Value depends upon accuracy of data.

(b) Econometric Models:

Econometric models are built up on the basis of analysis of past statistical data establishing the relationship between variables in a mathematical formula. The variables are those factors such as production, sales, finance and other activities affecting human resource requirement. Econometric model is used to forecast human resource requirements based on various variables.

(c) Bureks Smith Model:

Elmer Bureks and Robert Smith have developed a mathematical model for human resource forecasting based on some key variables that affects overall requirement for human resources of the organisation. They have given an equation.

En = (Lagg + G) 1/x/ y

Where En = Estimated level of demand for employees

Lagg = Turnover or overall current business activity

G = Total growth in business activity anticipated thought period 'n' in term of rupees

x = Average productivity improvement from today thought planning period.

y = Conversion figure relating today's overall activity to required employees.

This method is used when the values of G, x and y are accurate. To obtain the values of G, x and y different statistical techniques are used.

(d) Regression Analysis:

Regression analysis is used to forecast demand for human resources at some point of time in future by using factors such as sales, production services provided etc. This method is used when independent and dependent variables are functionally related to each other. Nowadays computers are used to solve regression equations for demand forecasting.

HR SUPPLY FORECASTING:

Supply forecasting means to make an estimation of supply of human resources taking into consideration the analysis of current human resources inventory and future availability.

EXISTING INVENTORY:

The first step in supply forecasting is to take a stock of existing HR inventory as follows.

(a) Head Count:

Count of the total number of people available department-wise, sex- wise, designation-wise, skill-wise, pay roll-wise etc.

(b) Job Family Inventory:

It consists to number and category of employees of each job family i.e. the jobs related to same category like office staff, sales and marketing staff, production staff, maintenance and industrial engineers, quality control engineers etc.

(c) Age Inventory:

It consists of age-wise number and category of employees. This gives us age composition of human resources. Dynamism, creative abilities innovativeness is present in young employees while making of proper judgment and display of maturity is shown by elderly employees.

Organisations prefer both young and old employees. Human resource planning should give due consideration to age-wise human resource mixing young and old employees in due proportions.

(d) Inventory of skill, experience, values and capabilities:

Organisation should take a stock of present inventory of skill, employees with number of years of experiences (10 yrs, 15-yrs, 20 yrs and more etc.), values and capabilities.

(e) Inventory of Qualifications and Training:

This consists of educational qualifications of the employees academic and technical and special qualifications if any and the training received by the employees.

(f) Inventory of Salary grades:

This includes pay and allowance-wise and total emoluments-wise stock taking.

(g) Sex wise Inventory:

Inventory of male and female employees of the organisation.

(h) Local and Non-Local-wise Inventory:

It includes the stock of local employees and the employees belonging to other areas such as different states of India.

(i) Inventory of Past Performance and Future Potentialities:

There are several human capacities or potentials required for performing jobs at the workplace. Requirement of these along experience needs to be taken into consideration while taking stock of human resource inventory.

LABOUR WASTAGE:

Labour wastage should be taken into account while making future forecast and find out the reasons of people leaving the organisation. Action can be taken to arrest the labour wastage and replacement of uncontrollable losses. HR manager must know how to make wastage analysis. For measuring permanent total loss due to labour the following labour turnover formula is used.

Labour Turnover Rate = Number of Employees left specified period (Say one year)/ Average Number of Employees during the same period x 100

HR Managers have to calculate the rate of labour turnover, conduct exit interviews etc. This helps them forecast, the rate of potential loss, causes of loss etc. The steps can be taken to reduce loss. HR Manager can calculate labour stability index by using the formula given below.

Labour Stability Index = Number of Employees with one year's service or more / Number of Employees one year ago x 100 By knowing all these labour instability can be arrested and labour turnover can be minimised.

The potential losses can be classified as permanent total loss, permanent partial loss, Temporary total loss and Temporary partial loss. Let us analyse these losses.

(a) Permanent Total Loss:

Permanent total loss is due to deaths, voluntary quits retirement, dismissals, retrenchment, and promotions out, demotions and transfers out. This can be filled in by new recruits, promotions in and transfers in.

(b) Permanent Partial Loss:

Permanent partial loss is due to loss of some skills, potentials and capabilities because of ill health or accidents. To get rid of this loss organisation can acquire new skill, knowledge, values, and aptitudes among the existing employees by providing adequate and necessary training.

(c) Temporary Total Loss:

Temporary total loss is due to loss of aptitudes, values, change in outlook and attitude of existing employees towards their jobs, department and organisation. Absenteeism is also a reason for this. This can be prevented by taking steps to minimize absenteeism to forecast loss of human resources due to it. Attitude of the employees towards organisation can be improved by knowing the causes of change and making efforts to remove those causes.

(d) Temporary Partial Loss:

This loss is due to consultancy or advice offered by the employees of the organisation to others. This loss of labour hours has to be there because many organisations encourage this practice as there is revenue to the organisations also.

If you think of revenue obtained by the organisations this loss to some extent is subsided. But these organisations not claiming from the fees or commission received by the employees, this loss is cognizable. After forecasting potential loss, potential additions are also to be taken into account.

POTENTIAL ADDITIONS:

Potentials added to the present inventory of human resources minimize the impact of potential losses.

Potential additions are of following types:

(1) Permanent total:

Permanent total additions are due to new recruitment, promotions granted to juniors, transfer effected from one department to another.

(2) Permanent Partial Additions:

These consist of acquisitions of new skills, knowledge, by the present employees. This will increase the stock of human resources in the organisation.

(3) Temporary Total Additions:

These consist of deputation of employees from other organisations. This will temporarily make additions to the stock of human resources.

(4) Temporary Partial Additions:

These come to the organisation through the consultancy and advice by the employees of other organisations.

SOURCES OF SUPPLY:

Estimation of supply of human resources depends upon internal and external sources.

Internal Factors:

Internal source of supply of human resources include the output from established training programme for employees and management development programmes for executives and the existing reservoirs of skills, potentials, creative abilities of the organisation.

External Factors:

External factors can be grouped into local and national factors.

(a) Local Factors:

Local factors include the following:

(1)   Population densities within the reach of enterprise.

(2)   Current and future wage and salary structure from other employers.

(3)   Local unemployment level.

(4)   Availability of employees on part time, temporary and casual basis.

(5)   The output from local educational institutions and training institutions managed by government and private establishments.

(6)   Local transport and communication facilities.

(7)   Availability of residential facilities.

(8)   Traditional pattern of employment locally and availability of human resources with requisite qualifications and skills.

(9)   The pattern of migration and immigration.

(10)   The attraction of the area as a better place to reside.

(11)   The attraction of a company as a better workplace and company as a good paymaster.

(12)   The residential facilities, educational health and transport facilities.

(13)   The regulations of local government in respect of reservation of backward and minorities communities.

(b) National Factors:

National factors include the following:

(1)   Trends in growth of working population of the country.

(2)   National demands for certain categories of human resources such as technical and management professionals, computer professionals, medical practitioners, technicians, secretaries, craftsmen, graduates etc.

(3)   The output from universities, technical and professional institutions.

(4)   Impact of changes in educational patterns.

(5)   Cultural patterns, social norms and customs.

(6)   Impact of government training schemes.

(7)   Impact of government policies in respect of employment regulations.

(8)   Migration and immigration patterns.

(9)   Impact of national educational facilities.

The net human resource requirement depends upon the human resource requirement of the organization for future i.e. demand forecasting and the total supply of human resources available.

■

CHAPTER – 9
WAGES AND INCENTIVES

ORIGIN OF WAGE

Wage is a reward for the services rendered or remuneration for the work done and it is as old as the society itself. In the primitive days, wages were paid in kind, most common of them was grains and the food. But with the advent of industrialisation wages form a complex problem and in almost all industrialised countries it became a sensitive area of public policy. Very soon the quantum of wages assumed a common cause of friction between the employers and the wage-earners. Frequent disputes between employer and wage-earners resulted in strikes over the demand for wage-increase. The determination of adequate wages that should be justifiably payable to die workmen by the employer, was not merely an economic problem but a multidimensional phenomena, necessarily involving relevant factors like place ot industry, prices of the product, living standards, basic needs of die wage-earner and the governmental policy in a given society. The natural instinct of the employer to keep the wage-bill to a minimum and workers struggle to secure a wage-increase to meet both ends, created a chaotic situation which demanded an immediate State's intervention to protect the weaker section of the society, namely, workers, in view of its low bargaining capacity.

DEFINITIONS OF WAGES:

Wages can be defined as a sum of money paid to the staff by the employer for rendering services as per a contract. In the ordinary language of the term wages implies 'reward' to the labourers for the services rendered by them. It may be paid daily, weekly, fortnightly, monthly, per hour or per unit. Services rendered by the labourer include both physical and mental services.

In the words of **Benham:** *"Wages are a sum of money paid under contract by an employer to a worker for services rendered."*

According to **ILO,** *"Wages refer to that payment which is made by the employers to the labourer for his services hired on the conditions of payment per hour, per day, per week or per fortnight."*

According to **Minimum Wages Act 1948,** *"wages means all remuneration, capable of being expressed in terms of money, which would, if the terms of the contract of employment, were fulfilled, be payable to a person employed in respect of his employment or of work done in such employment".*

CLASSIFICATION OF WAGES

Subsistence Wage: - The wage that can meet only bare physical needs of a worker and his family is called subsistence wage.

Minimum Wage: - Justice Higgin propounded the concept of minimum wage as the irreducible level of wage paid to an unskilled worker, considering him a human being living in a civilised society. In this single sentence, he indicated three important considerations, namely, (i) that minimum wage is an irreducible level which cannot be further reduced; (2) secondly, it is paid to an unskilled worker who has not undergone any expensive training to acquire skill, (3) thirdly, the worker is to be considered a "human being living in a civilised society and therefore he is entitled to same basic needs of food, clothing and shelter which any other human being requires. Thus according to Justice Higgins a minimum wage is that irreducible wage, which should enable the worker to get three basic necessities of life, namely, food, clothing and shelter.

Further expanding his concept, Justice Higgins described the essential components of the three basic needs of food, clothing and shelter and said that the food does not merely mean any stuff to satisfy the hunger, should have the essential nutritious value to retain the health of worker preserve his efficiency as worker. Medically speaking, a normal human body daily needs 3,500 calories in his food to retain his health. Therefore a wage which does not provide for a quality of food containing 3,500 calories cannot be strictly described as minimum wage.

Similarly clothing does not refer to anybody-covering but it should be sufficient to protect the workers from the severity of seasons, say soft clothing in summer and warm clothing in winter. It should also satisfy the natural instinct of the wearer to be respected in the society as he is considered a human being living in a civilised society. Thus the moral responsibility is also imposed on the civil society.

Thirdly the shelter is also further required to be sufficient to accommodate the family of the worker comfortably and it should not be a den to dump the workers' family therein.

Fair Wage: - Fair wages is an adjustable step that moves up according to the capacity of the industry to pay, and the prevailing rates of wages in the area of industry.

Living Wage: - Having described the minimum wage to provide for food, clothing and shelter as a basic and irreducible level of wage, Justice Higgins developed his concept of living wage as one which should not only provide for food, clothing and shelter but for some frugal comfort of life, good education to children, some amusement and provision for sickness and old-age including some measure of social security. Again die frugal comfort should be such as measured at the changing values at a given time. Thus according to Justice Higgins "Living Wage is one appropriate for the normal needs of the average employee, regarded as a human being living in a civilised society. It must provide not merely for the absolute essentials such as food, clothing and shelter, but for a condition of frugal comfort estimated by current human standards".

FACTORS INFLUENCING WAGES:

Determination of fair and adequate wage for a particular job is very difficult. Wages should be fixed in such a way which founds satisfactory both for workers and management.

Some of the factors which influence the wage rates are:

1. Demand and Supply of Labour:

Demand and supply is one of the important factors which influence the wage rates. If the number of workers required is more than availability of workers, then employees will be paid higher rate of work and vice versa.

2. Legal Provisions:

The government had made cretin laws/acts for fixation of minimum wages to the workers such as minimum wages act 1948. According to this act, the employer must pay minimum wages to the worker. If any employers do not follow the rule of this act, an action can be taken against him.

3. Ability to Pay:

Payment of wages also depends on the ability of a company to pay. A company running into losses will not be in a position to pay more than minimum wages, whereas a profit making company can give workers a share in the profit.

4. Nature of Job:

Wages also depends upon the worker's skill and the conditions of work. Some jobs can be done by skilled employees while some jobs can be done by unskilled employees. The work conditions can be safe or hazardous. So wages can be high or low, depending upon the worker's skill and conditions of work.

5. Working Hours:

Wages also depends upon the number of hours worked per day and the number of holidays.

6. Comparative Wage Levels:

Wage rates also depend upon the wages paid in competitive firms for the same type of work. Wages are therefore fixed after conducting wage surveys.

7. Cost of Living:

Cost of living also determines the wage rates. Wages should be such which satisfies the minimum needs of workers.

8. Type of Employment:

Wages depends upon the type of employment i.e. regular employment or contractual employment. A regular and permanent job provides security of service.

METHODS OF WAGE PAYMENT

The following points highlight the top three methods of wage payments. The methods are: 1. Time Rate System, 2. Piece Rate System, 3. Incentive Wage System

1. TIME RATE SYSTEM:

Under this method of wage payment, the workers are paid the wages on the basis of time. In this system of wage payment, the workers are paid the wages on the basis of time as, per hour, per day, per week, per fortnight or per month etc. This system does not consider the production of the employees during this time.

The amount of wages under this system is calculated as under:

Wages = Time spent by the worker × Rate of wages according to time.

For example, If the worker is paid at the rate of Rs.20 per hour and he spends 50 hours during a week, the weekly payment is: 50 x 20 = Rs.1000 per week.

Suitability of Time Rate System:

This system of Wage Payment is particularly suitable in the following circumstances:

1. When it is not possible to measure the production in terms of units or in any other terms
2. When the work is of high standard.
3. When it is not possible to divide the production into units.
4. When the production is of the nature that it requires efficiency more than the speed.
5. When the worker is under training.

Merits of Time Rate System:

1. Simplicity:

It is very easy to calculate the amount of wage under this system.

2. Certainty of the Amount of the Remuneration:

This system of wage payment provides certainty of the amount of wage payment to the employee. It develops the feeling of confidence and certainty among them.

3. High Quality of Production:

As this system of wage payment has no concern with quantity of production, quality of production produced by the workers under this system is very high.

4. Proper Utilisation of the Factors of Production:

As this system is not related with speed, the workers perform their work in very confident manner. They make the best Utilisation of the factors of production.

5. Co-Operation between Labour and Capital:

This system of wage payment brings the industrial peace because it satisfies the workers and the industrialists. Thus, it develops harmony and cooperation between labour and capital.

6. Best System for Artistic Work:

This system of wage payment is most suitable for artistic work.

7. Co-Operation and Unity of Workers:

As all the employees doing the work for same nature get the same amount of wages, this system develops the feeling of co-operation and unity among the workers.

8. Suitable for the Health of Workers:

This system of wage payment is suitable from the point of view of health of workers.

Demerits of Time Rate System:

1. Need of Intensive Supervision:

This system requires intensive supervision over workers. It increases the cost of supervision.

2. Lack of Incentive:

This system of wage payment makes equal payment to both the efficient and inefficient workers. Therefore, efficient workers do not get any incentive for more production.

3. Encouragement of Labour Unions:

This system encourages labour unions. Sometimes, these labour unions misuse their powers.

4. Misuse of Time by Workers:

Under this system of wage payment, the workers do not make proper Utilisation by their time.

5. Fall in the Quantity of Production:

Under this system of wage payment, the quantity of production decreases because the workers do not get any incentive for increasing the production.

6. High Cost of Production:

As the production is low and the payment to the worker is more, this system increases the cost of production.

7. It Kills the Efficiency of Workers:

As this system does not make any difference between efficient and inefficient workers, it kills the efficiency of efficient workers.

8. Increase in Cost Per Unit:

This system increases the cost per unit of production. Under this system, the cost per unit of production is uncertain because the quantity of production differs from time to time.

9. Difficult to Measure the Efficiency:

Under this system of wage payment, it is very difficult to measure the efficiency of workers because all the workers of equal status are paid the wages at equal rate.

2. PIECE RATE SYSTEM:

Under this system of wage payment, the workers are paid the wages on the basis of quantity and quality of work performed by them. Under this system, the rates of wages are determined according to quantity and quality of work and the workers are paid according to these rates.

The amount of wages to be paid to a worker under this system is calculated as under:

Wages = Units of production × Rate per unit.

For example, If a worker produces 100 pieces per day and he is paid at the rate of Rs.1.2 per piece, the daily wage is 100 x 1.2 = Rs.120.

Suitability of Piece Rate System:

This system of wage payment is very suitable in the following conditions:

1. When the work is of standard nature.

2. When the work can be measured easily.

3. When there is a great need of increase in the production.

Merits of Piece Rate System:

1. Incentive to More Work:

This system encourages the workers to do more and more work because they get their wages according to their work.

2. Proper Utilisation of Machines:

Under this system, the workers use their machines and equipment with proper care because they feel that if their machine is out of order, their work will be held up and their wages will be low.

3. Increase in the Quantity of Production:

The system of wage payment gets more production because all the workers make their best efforts to increase the production.

4. Best Utilisation of Time:

As the workers are paid according to their work, they make the best possible utilisation of their time. They do not want to waste their time.

5. Decrease in the Cost of Production:

This system decreases the cost of production because the maximum production is done by the workers in the minimum time. It decreases the cost per unit of production also.

6. Decrease in the Cost of Supervision and Administration:

This system of wage payment minimises the needs of supervision. It reduces the cost of supervision.

7. Easy and Simple:

This system of wage payment is very easy to understand and very simple to calculate.

8. Improvement in the Standard of Living of Workers:

Workers get more wages because they produce more. It increases their efficiency and productivity. It increases their remuneration also which improves their standard of living.

9. Mobility of Workers:

This system of wage payment increases the mobility of workers because they can change their enterprise easily.

10. Measurement of the Efficiency of the Workers:

This system provides an opportunity to measure the efficiency of the workers. It makes proper distinction between efficient and inefficient working staff of the enterprise.

11. Justified:

This system of wage payment justified also because the workers are paid the wages according to the work performed by them.

12. Helpful in Maintaining Industrial Peace:

This system brings industrial peace also because it satisfies both the workers and the employer.

Demerits of Piece Rate System:

1. Lack of Unity among Workers:

This system lacks the unity and mutual co-operation among workers. They feel themselves competitor to each other.

2. Loss of Workers on the Failure of Machines etc.:

It because of any reason, the machines fail or the power fails, the work of workers is held up and they lose their wages.

3. Misuse of the Factors of Production:

The workers do not pay proper attention towards the factors of production. They only want to increase the speed of production.

4. Adverse Effect on the Health of Workers:

This system motivates the workers to do more and more work. It affects the health of workers adversely.

5. Low Quality of Production:

This system of wage payment does not pay any attention on the quality of production. As a result of it the quality of production falls down.

6. Unsuitable for Artistic Work:

This system is not suitable for artistic work because artistic work cannot be paid only on the basis of quantity of production.

7. Uncertainty of Wages:

As the amount of wages depends upon the quantity of production, the actual amount of wages to be paid is always uncertain. The workers also cannot estimate their remuneration in advance.

3. INCENTIVE WAGE SYSTEM:

There are two basic systems of wage payment—time rate system and piece rate system. Both the systems have their merits and demerits. No system can be considered suitable for all times and under all circumstances. To maintain the merits of both the systems and to overcome the demerits of these systems, some experts have developed the systems of incentives wage.

These systems are also known as incentive wage systems, progressive wage system and bonus schemes etc. Under these systems, both the time and speed are considered as the basis of wage payment.

These systems provide incentives to the workers to produce more and more maintaining the quality as well. The workers are paid bonus or premium for the additional work. It is important to note that almost all the systems incentive wages provide for minimum guaranteed wages to the workers.

Characteristics of an Ideal Incentive Wage System:

Important characteristics of an Ideal Incentive Wage System are as under:

1. It must be easy to calculate and to understand.
2. The standards of work must be determined on scientific basis.
3. It must establish direct relationship between efforts and remuneration.
4. It must give a guarantee of minimum wage to all the workers.
5. It must be in the interests of both the employers and the employees.
6. It must be flexible but stable.
7. It must be framed in the manner so that it may be used widely for all the activities of the enterprise.
8. It must be helpful in increasing the production as well as productivity.

Advantages of Incentive Wage System:

i. There is increase in the prospect of workers to earn more. As shown by F. Herzberg good salary is one of the hygiene factors in the absence of which people are unhappy and dissatisfied. Wage incentive offers them the prospect of earning more.

ii. The scientific work study which is done before introducing a wage incentive plan brings about improvements in methods, workflow, and man-machine relationship and so on.

iii. There is effective reduction in the supervision costs Closer supervision of employees becomes unnecessary because workers become more responsible. Rather than the supervisor chasing the workers the workers themselves sometimes chase the supervisor for materials, tools, etc.

iv. Employees promptly expose all such problems before management which retard their earnings. Management becomes more alert in areas such as flow of process materials, adequate spares, etc.

v. Employees are encouraged to become "inventive". They invent and adopt ways and means to achieve their production targets with lesser exertion and lesser expense of energy. They come forward with new ideas and suggestions.

vi. There is improvement in discipline and industrial relations. Go-slow and similar other techniques are not resorted to by the workers to express their dissatisfaction with management policies and practices. There is increase in workers' punctuality and decrease in absenteeism.

vii. There develops a feeling of mutual co-operation among the workers as their operations are interdependent and any hold-up at one point may affect the production and earning at other points.

Effects of Incentive Wage System:

Experience has shown that incentive compensation is not an unmixed blessing. It may produce certain ill-effects unless precautionary steps are taken to check them in advance.

These ill-effects are as under:

i. There is tendency among the workers to sacrifice quality for the sake of quantity. This calls for a very strict system of checking and inspection.

ii. In the absence of adequate provisions incentive payment brings about certain rigidity in the operations. This makes it difficult for the management to revise norms and rates following changes in technology, methods, machines, materials etc.

iii. Employees very often ask for compensation whenever production flow is disrupted due to the fault of management.

iv. Unless greater vigilance is exercised there is a danger of workers disregarding safety regulations.

v. Unless a maximum ceiling on incentive earning is fixed some workers tend to overwork and undermine their health.

vi. Jealousies may arise among workers because some are able to earn more than others. In the case of group systems, the fast workers may be dissatisfied with the efforts of the slower members of the group; where heavy work is involved older workers in particular are likely to be criticised for being too slow. One likely effect of this is the splitting up of trade unions.

vii. The introduction of a system by results increases the amount and cost of clerical work since it involves considerably more bookkeeping. This is particularly true when the production is subdivided into many processes.

INCENTIVES: MEANING, DEFINITION AND ADVANTAGES

Anything that can attract an employee's attention and motivate them to work can be called as incentive. An incentive aims at improving the overall performance of an organization. Incentives can be classified as direct and indirect compensation. They can be prepared as individual plans, group plans and organizational plans.

Definition:

1. According to **Milton L. Rock**, 'incentives are defined as 'variable rewards granted according to variations in the achievement of specific results'.

2. According to **K. N. Subramaniam**, 'incentive is system of payment emphasizing the point of motivation, that is, the imparting of incentives to workers for higher production and productivity'.

3. The **National Commission of Labour** defines incentive as follows: 'wage incentives are extra financial motivation. They are designed to stimulate human effort by rewarding the person, over and above the time rated remuneration, for improvements in the present and targeted results'.

Types of incentives:
Incentives can be classified into three categories:
1. Financial incentives:

Some extra cash is offered for extra efficiency. For example, profit sharing plan and group incentive plans.

2. Non-financial incentives:

When rewards or prizes are provided by the organization to motivate the employees it is known as non-financial incentives.

3. Monetary and non-monetary incentives:

Many times, employees are rewarded with monetary and non-monetary incentives that include promotion, seniority, recognition for merits, or even designation as permanent employee.

Advantages of incentive Plan:

1. Incentive plans motivate workers for higher efficiency and productivity.

2. It can improve the work-flow and work methods.

3.   Incentive plans make employees hardworking and innovative.

4.   When employees are dedicated, supervision costs can be reduced.

5.   The National Commission on Labour says that under our conditions, wage incentives are the cheapest, quickest, and sure means of increasing productivity.

6.   Incentive plans help establish positive response in an organization.

7.   It helps workers improve their standard of living.

8.   The other benefits offered by incentive plans are reduced turnover, reduced absenteeism, and reduced lost time.

Disadvantages of Incentive Plan:

1.   Incentive plans can lead to disputes among workers, since some earn more than others.

2.   Hunger for money among the workers forces them to overwork, which may affect their heath.

3.   Some workers may involve in malpractices in order to earn more money.

4.   For enhanced incentives, they may sacrifice quality.

5.   It also leads to corruption by falsifying the production records.

6.   Incentive plans can create tensions among different personnel.

INCENTIVES IMPROVE PRODUCTIVITY

According to Caruth, Middlebrook and Frank (1982), the general purpose of incentive schemes is to increase productivity in the organization. By relating compensation to output, an employer is attempting to induce workers to turn out a greater volume of work thereby lowering the cost of producing a single unit of output. Specifically, the purpose of incentives to both an employee and the organization is to improve productivity and growth of the organization. It can be explained through following points:

1. Incentive improves motivation of the employees and hence improve productivity.
2. Incentives increase performance of the workers and performance leads to productivity.
3. Incentives recognize differences in employee performance.
4. Incentives increase competition among employees and hence improve productivity.
5. Incentives attract and retain productive employees.
6. Incentives reduce absenteeism and hence improve productivity.
7. Incentives motivate employees to reduce idle time.
8. Incentives objective is to reduce or control costs.
9. Workers utilize equipment more effectively and hence improve productivity.
10. It create positive attitude and employees work hard for the organization.

■

CHAPTER –10
ECONOMICS OF DISCRIMINATION

Discrimination in the labour market occurs when employers make decisions on wages and employment based on prejudices, such as race, gender, religion. It can lead to variations in wages for the same job and different employment rates.

Kenneth Arrow defined discrimination as:

"The valuation in the market-place of personal characteristics of the worker that are unrelated to worker productivity."

For example, employers refusing to employ people from ethnic minorities or paying women lower wages for comparable work.

In 1968, 850 women machinists at the Ford factory in Dagenham went on strike over equal pay. They received 87% of men's' wages. But, they argued their job was as skilled as the men. After a strike, Ford increased wages of the women to 92% of men's. It also contributed to the Equal Pay Act of 1970, which prohibited preferential wages on the grounds of gender.

Discrimination and the effect on the demand curve (Figure-10.1)

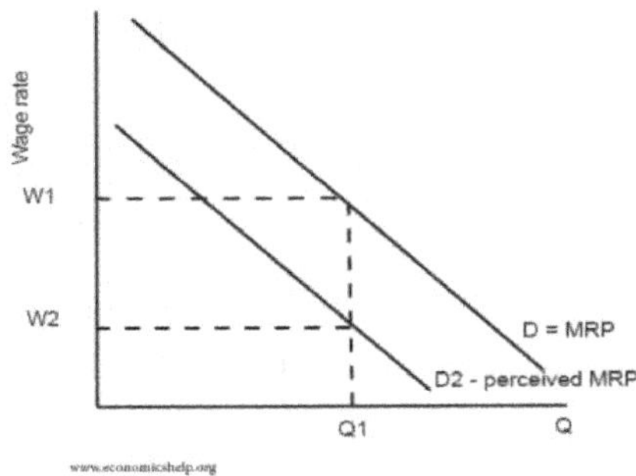

D=MRP shows marginal revenue product of workers. However, because of discrimination and employers preferences to avoid certain groups of workers, the 'perceived' MPR of that group is lower than it actually is. This group will not be employed at W1 and will have to accept lower wages.

Problems of discrimination

1. Discrimination leads to deadweight welfare loss. Certain groups of workers may be out of work or have a wage less than their marginal revenue product.
2. If firms have monopoly/monopsony power, discrimination enables firms to cut costs and receive more profits (at the expense of workers).
3. However, in competitive markets, firms will tend to experience higher costs as a result of discrimination – leading to higher prices for consumers.
4. Discrimination causes a sense of alienation, frustration and injustice. It can lead to social disorder with those discriminated on going on strike for better conditions.

How market forces can work against discrimination

If we have a competitive labour and product market, there are profit incentives working against discrimination.

- If a company wanted to employ only white workers, it would push up the wages for white workers and increase its cost of production.
- However, the company would then be vulnerable to another firm entering the market and employing ethnic minorities. If ethnic minorities have been discriminated against, their average wages would be lower. The new company could then pay lower wages than the discriminatory firm and undercut its rival.

- The firm who discriminates against ethnic minorities is, therefore, penalising itself. Market forces would put pressure on the discriminatory employers to cut wages and employ all workers.
- In theory, this should put downward pressure on wages for 'preferred' groups of white workers and lead to equalising pressures.

Gary Becker *The Economics of Discrimination (1955)* was an influential work in proposing this 'neo-classical' model of discrimination based on supply and demand.

Example – Discrimination against Communist film producers

In the 1950s, many film producers, such as Dalton Trumbo were banned from working in Hollywood because of the Communist beliefs. But, profit-making Hollywood studios started to find ways around these bans by secretly employing Communist script writers. The movie companies could pay lower prices to the blacklisted authors. The writers were happy to gain employment – even at a wage less than their MRP (Dalton Trumbo gained two Academy Awards whilst working as an anonymous script writer Roman Holiday and Brave One.)

When the market fails to end discrimination

The market can fail to end discrimination if:

- Government legislation enforces discrimination (apartheid laws US, South Africa)
- Discrimination occurs amongst consumers too.
- If firms have monopoly power – despite higher costs of discrimination, barriers to entry prevent new non-discriminatory firms from entering the market.
- Discrimination – pre-labour market. One major cause of wage differentials is not discrimination by employers but different life chances and education of people entering the labour market. If black-Americans have fewer qualifications than

average, economic theory would predict that even with non-discriminatory employers, average wages would be lower for certain groups.

Dual discrimination – employers and consumers

Suppose there is a market for private maths tuition. Companies may discriminate against female maths tutors and be less willing to employ women and/or pay lower wages. As a consequence, the pay for female tutors would be lower than male tutors and relatively higher for male tutors.

For a firm who didn't discriminate, there would be an opportunity to gain lower costs by employing female maths tutors. There is a profit incentive to avoid discrimination. However, suppose the prejudice against female maths tutors was also prevalent amongst customers. In this case, a firm employing female maths tutors may have difficulty selling their services – so the cost benefits of lower wages are lost.

In this case, the market fails to end the discrimination because the racism/sexism isn't just amongst employers but also consumers.

Example – First Female Doctor in the UK

In 1865, **Elizabeth Garret Anderson** opened up a medical practice in London. She was the first female qualified doctor in the UK. For the first six months, she struggled to attract patients due to lingering suspicions about female doctors – even though her prices were relatively cheap. However, in 1865 there was a cholera epidemic affecting both rich and poor. In the crisis, the desire to see a doctor suddenly outweighed prejudice about gender and in 1866, she saw 3,000 new patients. Anderson broke down discrimination on grounds of gender.

Example – Turn of Century Streetcar Apartheid in the US

At the turn of the century, in the south of the US, laws were passed to segregate streetcars into black and white sections. This included the Streetcar Segregation Act of 1903 (known popularly as Jim Crow laws)

These laws reflected racism of the time. But, many streetcar companies in Augusta, Savannah, Atlanta, Mobile, and Jacksonville, were reluctant to enforce segregation laws for as long as fifteen years after their passage because the laws diminished their profitability.

- Black and white areas led to more empty seats as sometimes empty seats were assigned to one group but then couldn't be used.
- Black customers tried to boycott streetcars and find alternatives.
- Not all white customers wanted to move to white-only areas. In fact, bus companies reported Companies had previously set up smoking and non-smoking areas. This discrimination was generally liked by non-smokers, but with additional segregation on race, non-smoking sections were no longer possible.

For over 15 years, companies in Memphis, Atlanta and Jacksonville often failed to implement these apartheid laws. Until government pressure meant the cost of resistance was greater than lost profits from segregation.

In 1955, **Rosa Parks** refused to give up her seat, starting the Montgomery Bus Boycott which led to many buses being idle for several months. Eventually, the economic pressure of the mass boycott caused bus companies to relent and segregation was lifted.

■

CHAPTER – 11
HRM AND HRIS

HUMAN RESOURCE MANAGEMENT (HRM)

Behind production of every product or service there is an human mind, effort and man hours (working hours). No product or service can be produced without help of human being. Human being is fundamental resource for making or construction of anything. Every organisation desire is to have skilled and competent people to make their organisation competent and best.

Human: refers to the skilled workforce in an organization.

Resource: refers to limited availability or scarce.

Management: refers how to optimize and make best use of such limited or scarce resource so as to meet the organization goals and objectives.

Therefore, human resource management is meant for proper utilisation of available skilled workforce and also to make efficient use of existing human resource in the organisation. The best example in present situation is, construction industry has been facing serious shortage of skilled workforce. It is expected to triple in the next decade from the present 30 per cent, will negatively impact the overall productivity of the sector, warn industry experts.

Human Resource Management (HRM) is a planned approach to managing people effectively for performance. It aims to establish a more open, flexible and caring management style so that staff will be motivated, developed and managed in a way that they can give of their best to support departments* missions.

Good HRM practices are instrumental in helping achieve departmental objectives and enhance productivity.

Edwin Flippo defines- Human Resource Management as "planning, organizing, directing, controlling of procurement, development, compensation, integration, maintenance and separation of human resources to the end that individual, organizational and social objectives are achieved."

According to **Decenzo and Robbins**, "Human Resource Management is concerned with the people's dimension in management. Since every organization is made up of people, acquiring their services, developing their skills, motivating them to higher levels of performance and ensuring that they continue to maintain their commitment to the organization is essential to achieve organsational objectives. This is true, regardless of the type of organization – government, business, education, health or social action".

Human Resource best practices

The first question is: what are HR best practices?

Best practices are a set of Human Resources Management processes and actions that work universally. In HRM research, there are two schools of thought on how to manage people. The first one is *best fit*, the second is *best practices*.

- The best fit school states that in order to add value, human resource policies should align with business strategy. This means that HR should focus on both the needs of the organization and the ones of its employees.

- The best practice school argues that there is a set of universal HR processes that lead to superior business performance. According to its proponents, there are certain bundles of HR activities that support companies in reaching a competitive advantage regardless of the organizational setting or industry (Redman & Wilkinson, 2009).

The Human Resource best practices presented below have been proposed by Jeffrey Pfeffer. Pfeffer wrote two books on this topic:

- *Competitive Advantage through People* (1994), and
- *The Human Equation: Building Profits by Putting People First (1998)*

In these books, he proposes a set of best practices that can increase a company's profit. When these best practices are combined (or bundled), their impact is even more profound.

These best practices are:

1. Employment Security

The first Human Resource best practice is employment security. There is a social contract between the organization and its employees. The organization asks employees to work, commit to the organization, and offer up their ideas.

Employees will only do this if they get something in return, like employment security. It enables employees to go home and provide for themselves and their families. This concept of security is essential and underpins almost everything HR does.

Employment security also benefits organizations because it helps them retain their people. When employees are laid off, for example, it's usually the organization that pays the price. They are the ones who have invested in the selection, training, and development of these employees. This is a costly process. If the organization doesn't work on retaining its people, they are more likely to leave and work for the competition.

2. Selective hiring

The second HR best practice is selective hiring. This enables an organization to bring in employees who add value.

You can't just hire anyone; you want people who are fit for the job. Companies do their utmost best to hire exceptional people because they add the most value to the business.

Research shows that the difference in performance between an average performer and a high performer can be as high as 400%! This holds true for different industries and job types, including researchers, entertainers, and athletes. Bringing in the right people is, therefore, a key to building a competitive advantage.

In today's digital world, there are a lot of different tools we can use to make the right selection. More and more companies vigorously keep track of their recruitment metrics to see how well they are doing in this regard.

Commonly used selection instruments are structured and unstructured interviews, IQ tests, personality assessments, work tests, peer assessments, and reference checks. These (pre-employment) assessments are used to uncover three key candidate characteristics.

1. **Ability**: is the person able to do the job? Does the person have the right technical and soft skills? Is the person smart enough to do the job well?
2. **Trainability**: can we train this person to improve his/her skills? Has the person the aptitude to learn and keep developing?
3. **Commitment**: will the person commit to his/her work and to the organization? Will we be able to retain this person once he/she is up to speed and fully productive?

3. Self-managed and effective teams

We all know that teamwork is crucial in achieving goals. High-performance teams are crucial for any company when it comes to achieving success.

Teams provide value because they consist of people who are and think differently but are working towards a common goal.

This means that different ideas are generated to help achieve the goal. These ideas are then processed and combined, resulting in the best ones being selected.

The best teams are cognitively diverse and psychologically safe. This means that team members can generate ideas that are different while feeling comfortable bringing these up and discussing them.

Creating and nurturing high-performance teams is one of HRs key responsibilities. Belbin's Team Role Inventory is a commonly used tool for team creation and cooperation. Individual personality assessments are also often used as they help to understand how other team members think and behave. Understanding these processes is one of the main responsibilities of a manager. This is the reason why a lot of management courses focus on it.

There are different tools that facilitate teamwork. Examples include communication software, feedback tools, project management tools, and other task and goal setting software. These can facilitate communication and help teams be more efficient.

Finally, HR needs to encourage different teams to work together in the organization. A team is usually part of a larger entity, like another team or a department. These larger entities also need to work together. Facilitating this helps to build an efficient and effective organization. One of the tools that can be used for this is Organizational Network Analysis.

4. Contingent compensation

Contingent compensation is the fourth Human Resource best practice. It has everything to do with compensation and benefits.

First of all, if you hire the right people, you want to compensate them above average. These are the people that will add the most value to your company so you want to retain them and pay them fairly. This is an example that shows how different best practices work together to provide more value than they would alone, in this case, selective hiring, contingent compensation, and employment security.

Paying people above the norm also has a number of potential disadvantages. For instance, it discourages bad employees to leave. However, if you're consistently hiring world-class performers, an above average compensation is a must. This sort of compensation can take the form of financial (base) pay and employee benefits.

Secondly, you want to couple individual rewards with the different types of contributions that employees make. These are performance-related rewards.

By coupling organizational performance outcomes with individual rewards the individual is incentivized to maximize this outcome. It also creates a sense of ownership for the employee.

Think of profit sharing, shared ownership, or stock options for instance. These are great ways to create employee commitment to the company's long-term vision and retain key talents.

In line with the previous, this type of co-ownership is usually not meant for all employees. Lepak & Snell (2002) offer a good model to assess how important individual employees are.

As an organization, you want to specifically retain your "Critics". They are people with unique skills (i.e. hard to replace) who are very valuable to the business. That's why senior managers, most of which fit this category, are often offered these benefits.

5. Extensive training

This HR best practice states that companies should invest heavily in training time and budget for its employees.

After recruiting the best people, you need to ensure that they remain the frontrunners in the field. This has become even more relevant today as the rate at which technology is developing is growing exponentially. This is where learning and development come in.

Figure-11.1

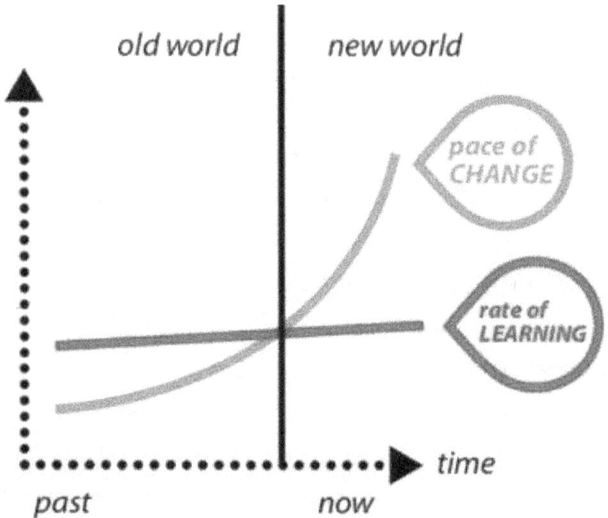

How do we create an organization in which the rate of learning matches the pace of change? Learning has become a way to stay innovative, grow faster, and sustain a competitive advantage.

Employers increasingly invest in skills-specific forms of training. According to the Economist's Lifelong Learning special report, the number of on-demand courses has grown exponentially. Thanks to the internet, everyone is connected and can learn anything, anytime, anywhere.

In addition to formal learning, on-the-job learning also plays an important role. Increased focus on feedback, coaching, and peer learning plays into this. This is part of the often quoted 70|20|10 rule:

- 70% of learning is from challenging assignments
- 20% of learning is from developmental relationships
- 10% of learning is from formal coursework and training

6. Reduction of status difference

This best practice in HR is rooted in the egalitarian practices of Japanese management. Although we just saw that some employees are more critical than others for the organization's success, this shouldn't be communicated in such a way. Every employee is a valuable member of the organization and should be treated as such.

In Japanese organizations, this is expressed with common canteens, company uniforms, and similar sickness and holiday entitlement. Such an egalitarian culture shows that everyone deserves equal respect and could help in promoting the sharing of ideas.

7. Sharing information

Information sharing is essential. This is an area where a lot of large companies struggle: How do you keep track of who knows what, so you know where to go to with your questions?

According to Pfeffer, there are two reasons why information sharing is so important. Firstly, open communication about strategy, financials, and operations creates a culture in which people feel they are trusted. It truly involves employees in the business. As an additional effect, it discourages hear-say and negative informal chatter. Secondly, if you want your people to share their ideas, they need to have an informed understanding of what's going on in the business.

Being informed about the business is also something that employees often mention as something they find important in attitude surveys, as well as having a chance to contribute to and influence decisions affecting their working life.

HUMAN RESOURCE INFORMATION SYSTEMS (HRIS)

Human resource information systems **(HRIS)** are software programs that allow HR professionals to store and organize vast amounts of employee information. These programs should allow management to access information and improve decision making.

There are many types of information systems (IS) on the market that perform a wide variety of tasks. One category of IS that is specifically designed to help human resource (HR) professionals in the course of their duties is called a **human resource information system (HRIS)** and is sometimes referred to as human resource management systems.

As the owner of Profits, Inc., your job is to oversee all of the operations of your growing company. You want your employees to be organized, so you go to the HR department to see what they are doing. In the HR department, you see people working on many tasks that relate to employee recruiting, hiring, pay and benefits, training, evaluation, and even attendance. Additionally, you want your management team to have the information necessary to make decisions regarding employees. Profits, Inc., is a service industry and your chief financial officer informs you that employee costs are the largest expenses that your company faces. As such, your goal is to do all you can to keep employee costs low.

HRIS Definition and Types

Your HR executive suggests that the company invest in an HRIS and explains that there are a number of types of HRIS that are made up by a combination of modules within the system - one module for each major task performed by HR personnel. One module may be dedicated to helping to receive, scan, email, and organize resumes to help sort through the many applicants that apply for each position within a company. Other modules may help a user to create an organizational chart or plan to find a replacement for personnel who are planning to leave or retire from a company.

The major function of the HRIS is to save time by taking repetitive functions and allowing one person to be able to do the work of many. For example, a company that has 1,000 employees, each of whom get paid every two weeks, would need an entire staff of people to compute the amount of taxes (federal withholding, social security, Medicare, state withholding, etc.), allotments, deductions, sick leave, vacation leave, and other factors for each employee. One module in an HRIS can automatically compute payroll information for all of the employees just by putting in the hours worked (for hourly employees) and whether there was any leave taken during the period.

You believe that managerial decision making is also a critical factor in choosing the specific type of HRIS. For example, Profits, Inc., employees are selected to perform particular jobs based on their training. Right now each manager has to either remember the training that each employee has or manually create reports that list each employee's training. If anyone else needs the information, they might need to go to five or six supervisors in order to get the information, and it may take a few days to do so. An HRIS could be loaded with the employee training data for many departments and would be able to produce a current training report within a few seconds.

Human Resources Information System is a system that lets you keep track of all your employees and information about them. It is usually done in a database or, more often, in a series of inter-related databases.

These systems include the employee name and contact information and all or some of the following:

department, job title, grade, salary, salary history, position history, supervisor, training completed, special qualifications, ethnicity, date of birth, disabilities, veterans status, visa status, benefits selected, and more. Any HRIS include reporting capabilities. Some systems track applicants before they become employees and some are interfaced to payroll or other financial systems.

An HRIS is a management system designed specifically to provide managers with information to make HR decisions. You notice that this is not an HR system...it is a management system and is used specifically to support management decision making. The need for this kind of information has increased in the last few years, especially in large and/or diverse companies, where decision making has been moved to lower levels, and large companies generally have the advantage when it comes to HRIS's...the cost to develop an HRIS for 200 people is usually close to that for 2000 people...so it is a better investment for large companies...larger companies tend to have systems that have a fair degree of customization.

Therefore, HRIS can be defined in simple words as given below. Human Resource Management Systems (HRMS, EHRMS), Human Resource Information Systems (HRIS), HR Technology or also called HR modules, shape an intersection in between human resource management (HRM) and information technology. It merges HRM as a discipline and in particular its basic HR activities and processes with the information technology field, whereas the planning and programming of data processing systems evolved into standardised routines and packages of enterprise resource planning (ERP) software. On the whole, these ERP systems have their origin on software that integrates information from different applications into one universal database. The linkage of its financial and human resource modules through one database is the most important distinction to the individually and proprietary developed predecessors, which makes this software application both rigid and flexible.

Advantages of HRIS

There are at least three reasons for installing such a system.

First is competitiveness: HRIS can significantly improve the efficiency of the HR operation and therefore company's bottom line. For example, W H Brady Company, a Milwaukee-based manufacturer of identification products such as labels reportedly cut several hundred thousand dollars a year from its HR budget through the use of HRIS. Software producer People-soft reportedly has a ratio of one HR staff to each 110 employees, a savings of millions of dollars a year when compared with the traditional ratio of one HR staff per 50-100 employees, and it credits that to its HRIS. The company expects the HR to employee ratio to shrink to 1:500.

Secondly, the HRIS can also bump the firm up to a new plateau in terms of the number and variety of HR related reports it can produce. Citibank for instance (now part of Citigroup) has a global database of information on all employees including their compensation, a skills inventory bank of more than 10,000 of its managers, and a compensation and benefits practices database for each of the 98 countries in which the company has employees.

Finally, the HRIS can also help shift HR's attention from transactions processing to strategic HR. As the HRIS takes over tasks such as updating employee information and electronically reviewing resumes the types of HR staff needed and their jobs tend to change.

There is less need for entry-level HR data processors, for instance, and more for analysts capable of reviewing HR activities in relation to the company's plans and engaging in activities such as management development.

Most HRIS Contain:

- Personal history - name, date of birth, sex
- Work history - salary, first day worked, employment status, positions in the organization, appraisal data and hopefully, pre-organizational information Training and development completed, both internally and externally
- Career plans including mobility,
- Skills inventory - skills, education, competencies...look for transferable skills

Operative Functions

The following operative functions are entrusted to the Human Resource Department to perform various works efficiently by taking proper decisions on the basis of Human Resource Information System.

1. Staffing & Employment, 2. Training & Development, 3. Wage & Salary Administration
4. Work Culture & Environment, 5. Security & Welfare Activities,
6. Employer & Employee Relation, 7. Records & Statistics,
8. Promotion & Transfer, 9. Integration & Separation,
10. Retirement & Retrenchment, 11. Legal Compliance & Government Reporting

Components of HRIS

The HRIS system will have five basic components namely

• Database

This stores all the information about the employee. Whenever new information comes in, it is entered in the database. In simple words, it is the store house of information.

• Data entry

The past as well as the new data is being entered into the database using the data entry tools. Security is being maintained for restricting unauthenticated entry of data into the database.

• Information retrieval

Whenever there is a need for information, it is retrieved from the database. The HRIS helps to retrieve combines information also.

• HRIC (Human Resources Information Center)

The staff responsible for day-to-day activities of the HRIS system and who are subject-matter experts.

• Data quality and integrity

It is ensured that the data retrieved is error free.

An HRIS system is made up of distinct yet interconnected modules that perform specialized functions. Each module is an "umbrella" term covering a group of related personnel activities. Some modules in a system may include some or all of these:

- Basic module containing basic, vital information.
- Career development module.
- Benefits module.
- Job evaluation module.
- Position control.
- Health and Safety module.
- Recruitment module.
- Payroll module.
- Employee self-service module.
- Training module.
- Labor relations module.

DEVELOPING HRIS

The development of HRIS can be explained through SDLC model (system Development Life Cycle Model).

I. Planning Stage

The development of HRIS starts with the planning stage. The planning stage involves two major steps namely

A.   Information Planning

B.   Systems Investigation

A.   Information Planning

Information planning involves development of long-range strategy, better utilization of HR/IS resources, better performance of HR functions.

This step involves the development of overall objective for the organization regarding the need of HRIS in the organization. The objectives of the various functional units were gathered and then the overall objective of the organization with respect to the HRIS is formulated.

The next step is defining the requirements. The statement of requirements specifies in detail exactly what the HRIS has to do. A large part of the statements normally deals with the details of the reports that have to be produced. Naturally, the statement also describes other specific requirements. This typically includes written descriptions of how users collect and prepare data, obtain approvals, complete forms, retrieve data, and perform other non-technical tasks associated with HRIS use.

This is followed by evaluating the present system and finding the need of the HRIS in the organization. This step not only evaluates the present system but also details the benefits of HRIS. In this step the resource requirements are analyzed.

This is followed by the identifying the HRIS projects available in the market. The priorities of the organization are set and the projects are analyzed against the priorities.

The one which meet the expectations will be selected.

The next step in this part is the identification of project team. The project team should consist of representatives from the

HR department, the accounting information department, representatives from user side, consultants and the system development department. The project team will be constituted and this team will set the schedules and the deadlines for the implementation of HRIS. They develop a detailed plan for HRIS.

System Investigation
The steps in investigation are
Stage 1 Selection
1. Forming an Investigation Team
2. Strategic Planning/Environmental Assessment by the investigation team
3. Feasibility Analysis which encompasses both economic and technical feasibility
4. Developing goals for System Development/Critical Success Factors
5. Submitting systems investigation report to the top level management on time
6. Getting the approval of the top management.

The investigation team and the project team can be one and the same. But in some cases, the investigation team is formed separately. Usually the investigation team comprises of persons from HR department, users, consultants, top level management.

The most important task in investigation is the feasibility analysis. The feasibility analysis has to answer certain questions like:-
What problems will automation eliminate or reduce?
How much will automation/HRIS cost?
What benefits can we expect?
What level of computer expertise exists in the HR dept?
What is the level of technical feasibility?
What is the level of economic feasibility?
What is the level of operational feasibility?

What is the level of schedule feasibility?

What is the level of legal and contractual feasibility?

The economic feasibility uses the cost benefit analysis. The tangible and the intangible costs will be taken into account. Similarly the tangible and the intangible benefits will also be taken into account. The technical and operational feasibility is all about the organization's ability to construct the proposed system. The project risk is assessed using information regarding project size, project structure, development group's experience with the application, user group's experience with development projects and the application area.

The operational feasibility assesses how a proposed system solves business problems or takes advantage of opportunities. The schedule feasibility assesses the time frame and project completion dates with respect to organization constraints for affecting change. The legal and contractual feasibility assesses the legal and contractual ramifications of new system.

II Analysis

In the analysis stage the main work to be carried out is the study of existing systems and their ability (or inability) to satisfy user needs/requirements. It involves the following steps:

1. **Assemble an analysis team**
   - Form team
   - Develop schedule for meeting objectives
   - List resources required at each stage
   - Establish milestones to monitor progress
2. **Collect appropriate data and requirements**
   - Identify data source
   - Collect data
   - Clarify the data

3. Analyze data and requirements

• Document Current Application Flows and Functionality

• Document Current Technical Architecture (if applicable)

• Conduct Needs Analysis/Business Requirements Definition

• Gap Analysis: Gaps between what we currently do versus what we want to do

• Revisit feasibility based on what is known about existing and desired system and potential solutions

4. Prepare a systems analysis report of the existing system and requirements

The inventory of the current systems like Payroll, Applicant Tracking, Performance Monitoring/Evaluation, Employee Maintenance, Compensation, Succession Planning, HR Planning, Training etc have to be analyzed and a report is prepared.

III Design

The design stage includes two stages namely the preliminary stage and the final stage. The final stage overlaps with the implementation stage.

The preliminary steps include

1. Finalizing Functional Requirements like which functions will be adopted for new systems

2. Finalizing Technical Requirements/Architecture which includes the selection of hardware and System Software, evaluating the available software and selecting the appropriate software. After analyzing the technical requirements, the organization will take the decision of whether to make the HRIS by itself or it can look for the vendor to purchase HRIS.

3. Acquire Hardware/Software

4   Technical Design

It includes the type of databases to be used, the screen shots, the flow of information, data security, data retrieval details.

5.   Reengineer Business Processes

- Work flow analysis
- Combining tasks
- Fewer controls at necessary points

IV. Implementation

In case of make decision, the final design is detailed and the system is built by the organizational personnel. In case of buy decision, the signs up the contract with the vendor and purchase the system from the vendor.

The implementation includes certain pre-requisites

1. Training

Training usually begins as soon as possible after the contract has been signed. First the HR members of the project team are trained to use the HRIS. Towards the end of the implementation, the HR representative will train manager from other departments in how to submit information to the HRIS and how to request information from it.

2. Tailoring the system

This step involves making changes to system to best fit the needs of the organization.

A general rule of thumb is not to modify the vendor's package, because modifications frequently cause problems. An alternative approach is to develop programs that augment the vendor's program rather altering it.

3. Data Entry to the system

Prior to start-up of the system, data must be collected and entered into the system.

The past data can also be entered into the system with the help of the system developers.

4. Testing the system

Once the system has been tailored to the organization's need and the data entered and a period of testing follows. The purpose of the testing phase is to verify the output of the HRIS and to make sure that it is doing what it is supposed to do.

5. Roll out

Start up begins when all the current actions are put into the system and reports are produced. If possible, maximum possible time can be devoted to check the working of HRIS. Even though the system has been tested, some additional errors often surface during start-up.

V Maintenance

Even after the new HRIS has been tested, it is desirable to run the new system in parallel with the old system for a period of time. This allows for the comparison of outputs of both the system and examination of any inaccuracies.

It normally takes several weeks or even months for HR people to feel comfortable with the new system. During this stabilization period, any remaining errors and adjustments should be handled.

A sound HRIS can offer the following advantages:

1. Clear definitions of goal.
2. Reduction in the amount and cost of stored human resource data.
3. Availability of timely and accurate information about human assets.
4. Development of performance standard for the human resource division

5. More meaningful career planning and counseling at all levels.
6. Individual development through linkage between performance reward and job training.
7. High capability to quickly and effectively solve problems.
8. Implementation of training programmes based on knowledge of organizational needs.
9. Ability to respond to ever changing statutory and other environment
10. Status for the human resource functions due to its capability for strategic planning with the total organization.

Critical Analysis of HRIS

Although almost all HR managers understand the importance of HRIS, the general perception is that the organization can do without its implantation. Hence only large companies have started using HRIS to complement its HR activities.

But HRIS would be very critical for organizations in the near future. This is because of a number of reasons.

- Large amount of data and information to be processed.
- Project based work environment.
- Employee empowerment.
- Increase of knowledge workers & associated information.
- Learning organization

The primary reason for delay in HRIS implementation in organizations is because of the fear psychosis created by "technology" and "IT" in the minds of senior management. They may not be very tech savvy and fear being left out.

But trends are changing for the better as more and more organizations realize the importance of IT and technology. Major HRIS providers are concentrating on the small and middle range organizations as well as large organizations for their products. They are also coming up with very specific software modules, which would cater to any of their HR needs. Hence HRIS would soon be an integral part of HR activities in all organization.

■

REFERENCES

Becker G.S. (1975), *Human Capital: A theoretical and empirical analysis, with special reference to education. (2nd ed.).* National Bureau of Economic Research. New York, NY: Columbia University Press.

Becker G.S. (1993), *Human Capital*, 3rd edition., University of Chicago Press, USA.

Bellante, Don and Mark Jackson, *Labor Economics: Choice in Labor Markets*, McGraw-Hill Book Company, New York.

Bhattacharya, Deepak K. (2006), *Human Resource Management,* (2nd ed.).

New Delhi: Excel Book Publisher.

Bouchard, P (1998), "Training and Work: Myths about Human Capital". In Scott S., Spencer B., and Thomas A. (Eds.), Learning for Life: Canadian Readings in Adult Education, Toronto: Thompson Educational Publishing, Inc.

Bowles, S. and Gintis, H. (1976), Schooling in capitalist America: Educational reform and contradictions of economic life. New York: Basic Books.

Campbell, R McConnel and Stanley L., *Contemporary Labor Economics*, McGraw- Brue, Hill Book Company, New York.

Gupta, S. and Gupta, S. (2008), *HRD Concepts and Practices,* New-Delhi: Deep and Deep Publication Pvt.Ltd.

Kempton, John, *Human Resource Management and Development: Current Issues and Themes*, MacMillan, London.

Khan, M. N. (1987), HRD In Modern Technological Structure. *Indian Journal of Commerce, XL*(150-151), p 83.

Mincer, J. (1958), "Investment in human capital and personal income distribution." *Journal of Political Economy* 66:4, p 281–302.

Mincer, J. (1974), *Schooling, Experience and Earnings.* New York: National Bureau of Economic Research.

Rao, T. V. and Pereira, D. F. (1986), *Resent Experiences in Human Resource Development* . New Delhi: Oxford and IBH Publishing Company.

Rao,T.V. (2012), HRD Audit: Evaluating the Human Resource Function for Business Environment, Response Book, p 17-18.

Richard B Perterson and Lam Tracy, *Systematic Management of Human Resources*, Addison Wesley Publishing Company, London.

Rubenson, K (1992), "Human Resource Development: A Historical Perspective". In L.E. Burton, In Developing Resourceful Humans: Adult Education Within the Economic Context, New York: Routledge.

Schultz, T. W. (1961), Investment in Human Capital. The American Economic Review 1(2), 1-17.

Schultz, Theodore W. (1981), *Investing in People: The Economics of Population Quality*, Hindustan Publishing Corporation (India), Delhi.

Smith Lisa (2014), Invest In Yourself With A College Education, Sept 11, *Investopedia.*

http://www.investopedia.com/articles/younginvestors/06/investin education.asp#ixzz4akKZoW00

Swanson, Richard A. and Holtan, Elwood F. (2008), *Foundation of Human Resource Development.* San Francisco: Berrett-Koehler Publishers. INC.

■